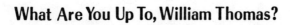

What Are You Up To, William Thomas?

What Are You Up To, William Thomas?

By
SUZANNE NEWTON

THE WESTMINSTER PRESS
Philadelphia

BOOK DESIGN
BY
DOROTHY ALDEN SMITH

First edition

Published by The Westminster Press®
Philadelphia, Pennsylvania

PRINTED IN THE UNITED STATES OF AMERICA

9 8 7 6 5 4 3 2 1

Library of Congress Cataloging in Publication Data

Newton, Suzanne.
What are you up to, William Thomas?

SUMMARY: In 1923 a mischievous fifteen-year-old boy
decides to start "applying himself" but just can't resist
one last prank.
[1. Humorous stories] I. Title.
PZ7.N4875Wh   [Fic]   77–23460
ISBN 0–664–32618–8

For Michele, Erin, Heather, and Craig,
who are always up to something

1

THE TELEPHONE RANG in the bookstore downstairs while I was fiddling with the rubber stamp in the Riverton Public Library upstairs. I waited a moment to see if it would ring again. If it did, that would mean Aunt Jessica was too busy to answer and I would have to go down.

When nothing happened, I went back to my work. I rubbed the stamp on the purple ink pad and tried it on a scrap of paper.

May 19, 1923.

That was the date, two weeks from now, when the books checked out today would be due.

"William!"

Aunt Jessica's voice floated up the narrow stairway —or maybe I should say "sailed" since nothing about Aunt Jessica floats. My heart took a dive. I had looked forward to settling behind the desk to read F. Scott Fitzgerald's *The Beautiful and Damned,* but no one ignored a summons from Aunt Jessica.

"William, I have to go out. Come down and tend the store until I get back! Is anyone in the library?"

"No'm." I checked once, to be sure of the page number, and made a note of it on the back of a card I kept in the drawer. Then I jumped up and sneaked the book back into its place on the shelves.

As librarian, Aunt Jessica has definite ideas about what fifteen-year-olds should read. *The Beautiful and Damned* is not it. Because of that, a good bit of the most interesting reading I do is on the sly.

"Are you coming, William?"

"Yes, ma'am. Right now."

She was standing at the foot of the stairs with her hand resting on the newel-post. Her wide figure, dressed in black, obstructed the way like a barge at the mouth of Riverton Bay. Her round, ruddy face was a little more flushed than usual under the wispy gray hair. She seemed disturbed, but then Aunt Jessica was often fretting about one thing and another.

"William, there's a business matter I must attend to immediately. I was putting those paper doilies and boxes of stationery in the window. The tags are right beside them." She pointed to some pink and blue boxes. "When you finish them, you can start shelving the shipment of new books in the box on the table in back. And mind you don't stop to read them!"

"Yes, ma'am." I almost sighed, but I have learned to control the sighing around Aunt Jessica. In some ways she is like an army general—she is not pleased by any show of constitutional weakness from the ranks. "What do you want me to do if someone comes to the library?"

"If it's someone you trust, don't worry about it. Let them check out their own books."

"What if I'm upstairs in the library with someone I don't trust, and someone else I don't trust comes into the bookstore?"

"Oh, for heaven's sake, William! You've worked here since you were twelve. How many times has that happened?"

8

She gave me a look that said, Don't be tiresome, and swept out of the bookstore with an umbrella in one hand and her large, bulky pocketbook in the other. I watched her through the plate-glass window. As she moved down the sidewalk she seemed to scoop up the air in front of her and cast it aside like a ship plowing through the ocean.

I have noticed when I'm walking with her along the sidewalks of Riverton that when men tip their hats to Aunt Jessica, their eyes become watchful. Mr. Marcus said once he thought she could read his mind when his head was exposed. And the women—even though they smile and say the right words—seem anxious to be on their way. Walking with her can make a fellow feel powerful.

Or lonesome.

The Riverton Public Library and Brassey's Book Nook are housed in the same building because Aunt Jessica was chiefly responsible for the town's having a library. She proposed a light public tax, enough to pay a librarian's salary and to purchase new books.

The only person who objected was Dr. Edgar Benson, who also happened to be the town's richest citizen. He gave a long speech in town meeting about the injustice of taxing people who were already taxed to the limit. When he sat down Aunt Jessica took the floor.

"Sir," she had said, "seeing that Riverton has no wealthy person willing to endow a public library, the town must take the responsibility."

Dr. Benson, it is reported, turned purple, but he couldn't say anything without getting himself in deeper. After all, *he* was the only person wealthy enough to endow anything. Eventually the people voted in favor of the library tax. That was before women had the vote, too, so Aunt Jessica had to be powerfully persuasive.

Shortly after the town fathers appointed her as first librarian, Uncle Alva died. The librarian's salary wasn't enough for her to live on, so she opened the bookstore. She offered then to give up the librarian's post, but the town council would not hear of it. All they asked of her was that she not let her private business interfere with public business.

Aunt Jessica was scrupulous about keeping the two separate. That was how I came to be employed at Brassey's Book Nook at the age of twelve. Actually, I worked in the library as much as I worked in the store, but I was officially Aunt Jessica's employee, obligated to be wherever she needed me most.

The doilies and boxes of stationery smelled like old-lady perfume, which discouraged me some. It isn't easy to make a bunch of little pale boxes look like something·you'd want to buy. I stuck price tags on them and arranged them in the window. Aunt Jessica says I'm better at it than she is, but I've told her not to let any of the guys hear her say that.

"Hey, Will!"

The words were muffled, coming from outside. I looked up. There was Bull Clammett, my so-called best pal, with his face and hands pressed against the glass. The tip of his nose, mashed flat, looked like a blob of white wax. He crossed his eyes and made weird gurgling noises.

"Hey, stop it!" I yelled.

His response was to exhale slowly. The vapor clouded the glass and his face disappeared. I went to the door and stuck my head out. Bull was just step-ping back to admire what he had done.

"Look," he said. "There I am, immortalized on the

front window of Brassey's Book Nook."

I looked. There were ten greasy fingerprints, the noseprint, a blob where Bull's freckled forehead had been, and two wavering rows of cracks where his chapped lips had rested. I ran back inside and came out with a cloth. It took me about thirty seconds to make him mortal again.

"You've erased me!" he protested.

"For a good reason! I don't like to stir up Aunt Jessica's wrath."

"I saw her go up the street," Bull said, following me into the store. "You aren't scared of her when she isn't even here, are you?"

"Heck, no!" I let the "heck" ring out loud and clear. Bull knows Aunt Jessica doesn't care much for that kind of language. "But she is my employer and she pays a good wage. I don't want to lose the job."

"Aw, you wouldn't lose your job if you burned the place down. She's your aunt."

Bull finds it hard to take that I get paid for shelving books and stamping little cards and tagging boxes, while he has to lug groceries up back steps every weekday afternoon and all day Saturdays. I must admit that looking at it from his point of view, I have a soft job. Sometimes I feel guilty about it, but not guilty enough to go looking for harder labor. After all, if Aunt Jessica needs me and is satisfied with the work I do, why should I quit? Or encourage her to fire me?

Bull sat down on a crate and watched me stack the boxes in the window. I expected some snide remarks concerning the sissy nature of the work, but none came. He just sat there. That is not like Bull, and so I began to feel uneasy. After a while he said, "I'm supposed to be delivering groceries."

11

"I wondered about that. Have you been fired?"

"No."

I waited for him to tell me whatever he had come to say. Bull is not a person to rush into things. I am always glad for him to drop in when Aunt Jessica isn't around. He is more than mere companionship. He knows everything that goes on in Riverton. If people here knew how proficient he was at gathering information, there is no telling what they would do, either to him or for him, depending on whether they had something to hide or wanted something to tell.

He claims he has bad adenoids and can't breathe through his nose, which accounts for his mouth staying sort of slack. That, and his vacant stare, which is probably due to nearsightedness, are real assets. When he is delivering groceries or doing odd jobs for people, they talk about things as though he were not a person at all, but some kind of working machine with no memory. Actually he is one of the more intelligent students in Riverton High's junior class. And he remembers everything.

"I picked up some interesting news about Paul Nisbett," he said at last.

I forgot the boxes.

If the population of Riverton had to be reduced by one, Paul Nisbett is the person I would vote to remove. He does not make my life—which is already difficult—any easier. For one thing, he is the best athlete in Riverton High School. He plays every sport but dominoes and has a 98.6 academic average. He is not just a member of the Forensic Society—he has managed to win the Declamation Medal for the past two years. He is a soloist in the glee club, an acolyte in the Episcopal Church. There is nothing he hasn't tried, and what is worse, nothing he has failed at doing, so far as I know.

I can't stand him.

Maybe he wouldn't bother me so much if Dad weren't forever holding him up in front of me as the Ideal. Dad works as bookkeeper for Mr. Nisbett at the Riverton Cotton Gin.

"Why can't you do thus and so, the way Paul does?" he says. Or, "You'd better shape up. Paul's going to go to college on his father's money, but you'll get there on your brains or not at all. Why don't you *use* them?"

Dad doesn't appreciate the uses to which I put my brain. Next year, at the end of my eleven years of formal schooling, I shall limp into graduation with barely passing grades, while Paul Nisbett—bless him —makes a full sweep of all the honors. But I shall have to my credit the longest list of successfully executed practical jokes in the history of Riverton public education.

It is a unique list. It includes the presentation of a collard sandwich to the president of the Latin Club, who thought he was getting a token of esteem from his fellow classmates. There was the staging of a shootout between two guys who smeared their shirts with catsup and lay down in the hall beside the principal's office one morning before first bell. And my favorite—a long-distance call from a person who said he was Cecil B. De Mille's producer and wanted to discuss using Riverton High School as the set for an upcoming movie. The principal was flattered and delighted—for a while. Imagine the color of his face after he had phoned the news to the state's largest newspaper and then learned it was all a hoax! Sure,

I could get good grades if I wanted—but let Nisbett have them. What else does he have to make up for his lack of imagination?

Bull, being my best friend, knows that I gnash my teeth when I hear the name "Nisbett," so I figured he wouldn't bring it up unless he had some information that would ease my perpetual pain.

"Well," I said, "what is it?"

"I just happened to be taking Miss Lauderbach's groceries out of the box while she was talking on the telephone. She was telling Mrs. Mellon that Nisbett's probably going to get the Douglas History Medal at this year's Commencement exercises."

My insides felt as though they were suddenly sucked out through a straw. Until that instant I had not realized how much I was counting on winning that medal myself. I had submitted what I thought was a superior essay on the role of the Belgian resisters in the Great War, but Nisbett had edged me out again. I was stunned.

When my brain began to work, I could feel anger coming on. I don't know who I was madder at—Paul Nisbett for grabbing the medal or Bull for telling me about it. Nobody was supposed to know the winner until Commencement anyway.

"Is that what you came to tell me—that Nisbett's getting the history medal? Do *I* care if Nisbett gets the history medal? So what else is new! Nisbett gets *all* the medals!" I strode up and down the aisles of the shop waving my arms and yelling. There was a knot in my throat and I knew if I didn't yell, no sound would come out. "Bring me some *news* once in a while! Tell me that *you* won the darn medal—or that *I* did!"

14

"I know how much you wanted it," Bull said, when he could get a word in. "I thought a long time before I decided to tell you. I didn't think it was a good idea for you not to find out until the very last minute. I— well, I thought you might go nuts and kill Nisbett right there in front of everyone at Commencement. I'm sorry to be the bearer of bad tidings."

I turned and looked at Bull. I didn't know he knew I wanted the medal. He even looked unhappy. I quit storming around and sat down beside him on the crate.

"Yeah," I said. "Yeah, you did the right thing." I took a deep breath to sort of loosen the knot in my throat. "I have to get used to it."

We both sat there for a minute or two pondering the injustices of this life. After a while Bull said, "Graduation is three weeks from yesterday."

"Yes, I know."

"A lot could happen between now and then, it seems to me." His words carried a peculiar weightiness.

"Like what?"

"Depends." Bull's slack mouth spread into a grin. "So what if Nisbett wins the medal? He could *lose* something too."

My brain went into high gear, which helped to ease the black, swampy feelings in my chest. What could Nisbett lose? The answer to that question could be the greatest joke of my career.

"Bull, that's terrific!"

Bull smiled modestly. He opened his mouth to reply, but about that time Mr. Marcus from the hardware store across the street stuck his head in the door.

"That your bicycle parked on the sidewalk, Bull?"

Bull jumped as though someone had stuck him with a spear. "Yes, sir!"

"Well, best go to it. Somethin' in that box has begun to leak through."

Bull slapped his forehead and ran. I watched him go with considerable regret. He was good for me. Whenever disaster struck—and in my life it frequently did—he was there to remind me not to reflect overmuch on the present troubles. Bull liked to move on. We had collaborated in some fine mischief as a result of his tendency to get up, dust off, and start again.

But this time it wasn't easy. Even with the prospect of finding a way to humiliate Paul to occupy my mind, I could not get rid of my disappointment. The Douglas History Medal, sponsored by our local newspaper, was being awarded for the first time this year, and I had dreamed of Dad's reaction when they called out my name as the first winner. I had been so *sure*. I had imagined him beaming, slapping me on the shoulder, shaking my hand, being amazed. Reality was bleak. I allowed myself a few hearty sighs, since Aunt Jessica wasn't around to hear.

Several customers came in while I was working, one of them Lilly Fentrice. Lilly is in my class, and ever since I have known her, she has been timid to the point of heart failure.

She crept into the store, looking all around like she expected to be swallowed by wolves. When she caught sight of me she turned pale and then pink.

"I'm going up to the library," she said in a soft, whispery voice.

"Sure, go ahead," I said. "Nobody's up there."

She looked so ridiculously relieved at the news that

16

it did something to me. I left my work and went over to her with my hands in my pockets and what I thought was a Valentino glint in my eye.

"On second thought," I said, "maybe I'd better go up with you."

Her eyes got large and dark. I leaned toward her. "What's the matter—scared I'll kiss you or something?"

She almost went to pieces right there.

"I'm not planning to kiss you," I went on. "But Aunt Jessica said I should go up with anyone I didn't trust."

She looked at me blankly at first, then her mouth formed an O and she stamped her foot. Lilly Fentrice actually put her foot down! I wasn't expecting it.

"Will Thomas, what do you mean! Mrs. Brassey trusts me absolutely, whether you do or not! And let me tell you, *I'm* the one who needs to worry. There's no telling what would happen if you went up to the library with me—"

She was really yelling. I heard the door open and close as someone came in. I wanted Lilly to hush but she was wound up. She was so angry she had forgotten to be scared. She had a rosy spot on each cheek and her brown eyes flashed. I was torn between my fascination for this new aspect of her, and the desire not to be caught causing it.

"William, what in the world is going on!" It was Aunt Jessica. I was never so glad to see her in my life.

Lilly began to change back to her normal self in Aunt Jessica's presence. I was relieved, though a bit sorry—I felt I was watching her become a photograph again after a few seconds of being an oil painting.

"I was just on my way up to the library, Mrs.

Brassey," Lilly whispered, looking down at the floor.

"Very well, go ahead," Aunt Jessica said. Her voice was kindlier than usual. When Lilly was safely out of earshot she turned to me. I tried to look her in the eye, but it is never easy to do when my conscience isn't perfectly clear.

"I presume you have done the tasks I gave you?"

"I finished the window. And I've been working at shelving the books."

She looked around the store, and then—of all things—Aunt Jessica sighed! It was unusual for Aunt Jessica to sigh in that quiet, discouraged way. Her sighs were ordinarily loud gusts of frustration and defeated purpose. The hairs on the back of my neck prickled.

"There's really no need for you to stay on today," she told me, peeling off her gloves. She went to the desk in the rear corner where she kept invoices and other business records. She sat down behind it and began to shuffle through some papers, as though she were looking for something.

It was definitely out of character for her to dismiss the hired help in the middle of the day on Saturday. My uneasiness grew. I followed her to the desk.

"Why not?"

She put on her glasses, which hung on a chain around her neck, and peered at me over them. "I just don't need you—that's why."

It was not the answer I had expected. I had a sudden vision of myself hauling large boxes of groceries up back steps for the duration of my youth.

"Oh," I said. "Well. In that case."

I just stood there, not knowing exactly what to do next. Two major blows in a single day. Lost the medal. Lost my job. Working hard—or hard enough

18

—at both, and where did it get me?

"William—"

I looked at Aunt Jessica and we locked eyes. And suddenly she had a sheepish expression on her face which I am sure only God and I have been privy to. She leaned forward and lowered her voice, as though she were going to mention s-e-x or underthings.

"William, I can't pay your wages anymore."

That was even more of a shock than losing my job. I thought that I had probably misunderstood what she said. Aunt Jessica got up suddenly and began pacing up and down. She was very upset. The little blue eyes got watery. She took a handkerchief out of her pocket and blew her nose loudly.

"I have to tell you this, because I wouldn't want you to leave thinking I was dissatisfied with your work. That is decidedly not true. You've done a splendid job ever since you began working here."

She had to stop and wipe her eyes and blow her nose some more. I just stood there with my arms hanging down, feeling awkward. It was unthinkable for Aunt Jessica to cry. Other women wept, but not she.

"I've just been to the bank," she said, when she could manage to talk again. "I'm in arrears in my payments on the loan they made me when I started the business."

I was aghast, partly at the notion of Aunt Jessica being in arrears in anything, badly as she hated to owe anyone money, but more at the fact that she would tell me. I didn't know what to make of it.

"You don't need to worry about that," I told her. "Dad will bail you out."

She gave me a funny, half-angry look and shook her head. "Your parents were very much opposed to

19

my going into business for myself. In your father's opinion, no woman has what it takes to make a go of it—least of all me. He vowed that if I failed, he would have nothing to do with my affairs—I should have to look after myself."

"Aw, he didn't mean it. He was just trying to scare you!"

"Perhaps," she said. "But I will not ask him for help, and I will thank you not to mention a word of this to him."

I didn't say anything. I didn't know how I could keep from mentioning it. After all, if she lost her livelihood, mine went with it. Besides, I felt that she was inclined too much toward stubborn pride.

"William?"

"Yes, ma'am?"

"Promise!"

"Aunt Jessica, I can't do that—"

"Well, then, at least wait a few days before you tattle. The bank has given me a reprieve while I look for a solution. It would make me very happy to be able to work it out myself. Your father is my dear brother, but he can be extremely pompous and self-righteous. I hate to hear him say 'I told you so.' "

I could appreciate her feelings in the matter. Then, too, it stung me to think that Aunt Jessica expected I would tattle. "I'll keep my mouth shut," I said.

"Thank you. I hope to get through this trying situation without embarrassing you or anyone else." Her eyes got watery again. "I don't know whether you are aware of it, William, but it is hard for a woman to get a loan from a bank. They require things of a woman that they would never require from a man of equal station."

20

"It doesn't seem fair—" I began.

"It's *not* fair!" She banged on the desk with an open palm. "I work hard. I pay my taxes. I have always paid my debts promptly. I daresay if your father had encountered this—this same difficulty, the bank would never have subjected him to such humiliating treatment!"

She blew her nose loudly again, and as though it were a summons, several customers came in all at once. There was no time to talk, and she said nothing further about my leaving. While I waited on the customers I pondered the strangeness of things. So far as I could tell, the Book Nook was prosperous enough. The average day's receipts had been enough to pay the rent and my wages, and naturally it was the wages that had concerned me most. I had assumed that Aunt Jessica was saving money. She certainly hounded *me* enough about putting aside a part of everything I earned against a rainy day. She herself had gone with me to the bank when I was six to open a savings account of my own, and she contributed regularly to it—a dollar for each birthday and for Christmas.

The last customer paid and left. I stood by the cash drawer and put the money in more thoughtfully than ever in my life. For the first time I noticed the amounts of the purchases that had been made. Five people had come and gone. The total receipts came to three dollars and forty-four cents. I let the pennies and dimes clink into their compartments one by one. It was nearly lunchtime, the cash drawer hadn't much in it, and a good portion of what was there had been put there that morning by Aunt Jessica for the purpose of making change.

"It isn't very encouraging, is it?" she said at my elbow.

I jumped. I thought she was still working at her desk.

"Oh, it isn't so bad!" I tried to sound hearty, but it was like telling a person who is about to die that he'll be up and around in no time. I closed the drawer with a bang and faced her squarely.

"What happened, Aunt Jessica? I thought we were doing fine."

She turned and went back to the desk and I followed her. She opened a drawer and took out a ledger.

"Alva left me very little when he died," she said, opening it to a certain page. "Schoolteachers don't make very large salaries, as you well know, and the little we had saved went to pay the doctor in his . . . last illness."

Aunt Jessica seldom talked about Uncle Alva. I watched her face, trying to discover how she felt about him. It was hard to imagine her ever being romantic about anyone.

"I knew the insurance money would be used up in less than two years, even if I were frugal. So I decided to invest it in a business of my own. That was my collateral when I went to the bank for the loan."

"You mean you had to borrow money anyway, even though you had the insurance?"

"Oh, yes. I still needed several hundred dollars. I wanted to make improvements in the store, and I had to purchase the stock."

"How much do you still owe?"

"Not a great deal. To those people at the bank it is a mere dribble, but it is quite enough for them to

22

take everything I own in payment—and they have a legal right to do so."

"You've been paying them back all along," I said. "Why can't you continue the payments if business has been about the same?"

"I've . . . had to use some of the money for a—for a special project." She would not look me in the eye. "Now, you mustn't get the idea that it was something foolish or dishonest, because it wasn't either of those things!"

If she hadn't been so serious, I would have laughed. Aunt Jessica would face a firing squad before she would do something dishonest. "Can you tell me?" I asked.

"No. Not without betraying a confidence. I wouldn't dream of it." Aunt Jessica drew herself up, proud and stubborn once more. I grinned in spite of myself.

"It's going to be O.K.," I said. "I feel it in my bones. And besides, Dad *will* bail you out if you need him. And you can move in with us if the going gets too rough."

"Heaven forbid!" she said, throwing up her hands. "I wouldn't live with either of your parents! Now— get upstairs and attend to the library. And mind you leave Lilly Fentrice alone. She's nervous enough without having to put up with your foolishness!"

2

AT A QUARTER OF SIX I left Brassey's Book Nook with a week's wages in my pocket. Although Aunt Jessica had tried to obstruct my view while she was counting it out, I saw that she had taken from the cash drawer almost everything that had gone in that day, just to pay me. That, more than anything else, made me realize the seriousness of things.

"Look," I said, putting my hands behind me, "you don't have to pay me."

"Nonsense. Hold out your hand."

"I'd rather not. Use the money to pay the bank."

Aunt Jessica drew herself up and gave me a withering look. "If I owed my very soul to the bank, I'd pay my employees first! Don't you think I know what is important?"

I held out my hand and she laid several bills and some coins in it.

"Pay your debts," she said, repeating the advice she gave me every week. "And save some for a rainy day."

"Yes, ma'am." I stuffed the money into my pocket and told her good night.

There were not many people out on the streets and sidewalks. Most had gone home to dinner, or, in the case of the farmers who came to town only on Saturdays, had started back earlier in order to arrive home before dark. I walked three blocks on Main, then turned right on Hildebrande, a narrow avenue lined with tall maples that met in an arch overhead. In summer it was a cool, green corridor; in winter, a skeleton archway, bare as marble and as elegant. The homes were huge and grand, with turrets and porches and curving bay windows. I rarely saw the people who lived in them, but the lawns were perfectly kept, the houses gleaming. It was clear to me that the rich did not sweat and yearn and stew like the rest of us. I was sure their lives were serene and uncluttered, like the grounds surrounding their mansions.

I thought about our house on Felker Street, with its yellow plainness and its narrow front porch with the token filagree around the banister. Someone was always coming or going—my brother, G.C., Jr., who worked at Marcus' Hardware; my mother; Dad; Lucille, who was Mother's washerwoman; any of Lucille's six children; and occasionally Aunt Jessica. Our house looked lived in to the point of rubbishness. Things were abandoned on the porch and in the yard. Anyone could see that no inch of space was left untrod upon or unused. The grass was careless about where it grew. I longed for the quiet spaciousness I saw beyond the stone and ironwork fences of Hildebrande. Nobody on that street worried about foreclosures or debts or having to move in with the relatives.

As soon as I turned the corner into Felker Street, I saw Dad sitting in the porch swing reading the evening newspaper. He still had on his hat—hard straw for the spring and summer—which made him seem more like a visitor than a permanent fixture. Whereas most fathers shed jackets and ties as soon as they got in from work, Dad stayed dressed until bed-time. He seldom looked rumpled.

He looked up when I came into the yard.

"Well! I wondered when you'd be home. Surely Jessica can't have so much business that you have to stay until six on Saturdays!"

"We did all right," I said.

"Lots of customers today?"

"About the same as usual." I started into the house. Dad folded the paper shut and followed me. I felt his presence at my back, heavy and questioning.

"Your mother has dinner ready. We were all wait-ing for you. Wash up and come to the table quickly."

"Yes, sir." I was relieved that he didn't ask any more questions.

Upstairs in the bathroom I washed my hands, an-ticipating Mother's usual mention of "those dirty li-brary books—no telling *who* has handled them!" I wet my hair, parted it in the middle, and slicked it down with a comb. My reflection stared back at me somberly. We did not look like Valentino. The nose was a little large, a bit too pointed. I wished that my neck weren't so thin, and that my hair was dark and straight instead of brown and inclined to curl. The lower part of my face was dark with fuzz which I wanted to shave, but I hadn't quite gotten up the nerve to ask G.C. to lend me his razor. I wasn't sure I could endure his teasing scorn.

"Will-yam?"

Mother's calling voice was different from her regu-lar, breathy, timid speech. Her brother teased her about learning to call her sons by practicing on the hogs on my grandfather's farm. It may have been true, but she did not like to be reminded that she had been raised on a farm. Marrying Dad and moving

26

into town had been a step up in the world for her. I think that she wanted to believe she had been a town girl all her life, enjoying teas and socials and observing the niceties.

"I'm coming!" I yelled, giving the fuzz on my chin one last inspection. It seemed very thick and dark. I decided to ask for the razor right after dinner.

Dad, Mother, and G.C. were sitting at the round table when I came into the dining room. The dishes of food were already placed, the steam rising in a fragrant fog. I sat in my usual place between Mother and Dad, across from G.C., and we bowed our heads while Dad prayed the Long Blessing. Other meals were blessed more perfunctorily, but the Long Blessing was for the evening meal and Sunday dinners. It did not always have the same words, but it passed through the same stages—praise, confession, petition, promise, and benediction. I had made those distinctions myself after years of observation and growling stomachs. When the prayer was done, Mother began serving plates.

I tried to catch G.C.'s eye, but he was thinking about something else. G.C. is four years older than I am. He started working at the hardware store when he was twelve. When he graduated from high school, Mr. Marcus offered him a full-time job. Nothing changed. He lived at home, ate Mother's cooking, paid room and board, and went to work every day. He never seemed discontented about anything—except me, maybe. Saturday evenings, as soon as he could gobble dinner and get slicked up, he was gone with some girl—hardly ever the same one twice, to hear him tell it. Dad conversed with him endlessly about such boring things as cost, capital, overhead, savings, principal, interest. It made me sad to see

27

how dull G.C. had become in the past two years. I could remember when we used to be pals and got in trouble together. In those days he would take the rap for both of us.

"Who came to the store today?" Dad asked. I thought he was talking to G.C., so I didn't even look up from the biscuit I was buttering.

"William, your father asked you a question." Mother's voice was full of apprehension. She has a great dread of scenes.

"Sir? Oh. Well. Gee, I don't know—Lilly Fentrice."

"Is that all?"

"Well, no. You want me to make a list?"

"You needn't be impertinent," Dad said. "I asked a civil question."

I put the buttered biscuit on the edge of my plate. "Mrs. Minway," I began, staring up at the ceiling light fixture for inspiration. "Walter Bleckenberg. Father Joseph. Lulie Bledsoe. Dan Fenwick. Mrs. Charlie Powell. Sallie and Annie Rodney—"

G.C. said a swear word and clattered his fork on the plate. Mother gasped and Dad glared, but he didn't get sent away from the table as I would have if I'd said a swear word. Perhaps that is one of the advantages of paying room and board.

"What difference does it make?" G.C. grumbled.

"Don't talk with your mouth full." Mother's voice quavered.

"Have I got to sit here and listen to this kid name every solitary soul that visited Brassey's Book Nook today?"

"It *is* interesting," Dad said to me, "that you can remember so precisely who came in on a busy Saturday."

"Yes," said G.C., giving me a scornful look. "Our store is so crowded on Saturdays that you can hardly move in the aisles. I couldn't name you ten people who were there today—they all blur together."

"Mr. Marcus has a thriving business," Dad observed.

I did not like the turn the conversation had taken. It led too directly toward the subject Aunt Jessica had told me not to mention. I searched frantically for a wrenching change of topic.

"People were looking for graduation gifts today. You know, Commencement is in less than three weeks."

"Oh, that's right!" Mother's small white hand went to her throat and I knew I was home free. "I have to get something for Anabelle's daughter who's graduating in Georgia."

I settled back to eating my biscuit.

"Ah, yes," said Dad. "Graduation. A memorable occasion. Especially if one has done well throughout one's school career."

The biscuit turned to dry crumbs in my mouth. I chewed very hard and kept my eyes down. Out of the frying pan, into the fire.

"I'm glad I'm not graduating this year," I said, when I finally managed to swallow.

"So am I," Dad replied. "Your prospects for the coming fall would be exceedingly dim."

I decided not to respond to that. When his tone became slightly acid it was better not to egg him on. I glanced at Mother. She was uneasy. Her hands played nervously with the frills at the neck of her blouse.

"You did submit a paper for the junior history

award, didn't you, William?" She thought she was helping me.

"Yes, ma'am."

"Well—have you heard yet whether you won?"

"They don't announce that until the night of graduation. Besides—"

"Besides, what?" Dad said.

"Besides—the newspaper sponsors the award—and you know Paul Nisbett's second cousin is editor."

"What does that have to do with it?"

I shrugged. If he didn't know, there was no use in my telling him.

G.C. didn't stay for dessert. He excused himself from the table and went up to his room. Shortly afterward I heard him go out the front door whistling. With him went my hopes for the razor. I wished that I had somewhere to go, especially if it were somewhere worth whistling about.

With him gone the house settled into a deep quiet. Not that he was all that entertaining, but when there was no one but Dad, Mother, and me, the place was like a mortuary. Dad took up the paper again and went to the living room. Mother retired to the kitchen. My choices were limited. I could go sit in the living room with Dad and answer probing questions, or I could go to my room. Sooner or later, he was bound to ask whether I had studied my Sunday school lesson. To postpone that moment, I reached over and picked up a book called *Devotional Meditations for Young People* that was gathering dust on Mother's sewing table. While I turned its pages, not seeing them, I wondered what Bull was doing. One thing for certain, he wasn't confined to his house on Saturday nights.

Paul Nisbett was going to win the Douglas History

Medal. In my mind's eye I saw the crowded auditorium at Riverton High School, smelled the air with its odor of gardenias and lavender, heard the sounds of paper programs rustling and the rumble of voices. The teacher in charge of awards would make much of the winner of that medal—even before she announced his name she would speak of his intelligence, his purposefulness, his mature judgment, and other attributes. And then she would call the name Paul Nisbett. And Nisbett, pretending modesty and surprise, would get up and go along the aisle to the platform, where Miss Lauderbach with a tender, proud smile would hand to him a small box—

Dad put down his newspaper and peered at me over the tops of his rimless spectacles. "What are you thinking about?" he asked.

It was like having someone fling open the bedroom door when you're undressed. "My Sunday school lesson."

That was not the answer he had expected. He cleared his throat, shook the paper, and folded it shut.

"I see. And what is the text?"

I looked up at the ceiling. " 'What man,' " I quoted, " 'if his child ask for bread will give him a stone, or a snake if he asks for a fish? If ye, then, being evil, know how to give good gifts to your children, how much more will your heavenly Father give good things to those that ask him.' "

"Very good," he said. "However, that was last week's lesson."

I focused on the floor a few inches in front of his highly polished black shoes.

"It made a deep impression on me," I said.

He made a funny noise in his throat. "This week's

31

lesson has the following text: 'Enter ye in at the strait gate: for wide is the gate, and broad is the way, that leadeth to destruction, and many there be which go in thereat: Because strait is the gate, and narrow is the way, which leadeth unto life, and few there be that find it.' "

It seemed to me that he was putting undue emphasis upon such words as "destruction" and "narrow."

"That's a very gloomy text," I said.

"Only for those to whom it applies," he replied sharply. "I advise you to find your quarterly and study the commentary."

That is how I came to be upstairs in my room reading detective magazines when the doorbell rang. It was highly unusual for anyone to come calling at our house on Saturday night. I slid off the bed and tiptoed to the head of the curving stairway. I couldn't see down into the hall below, but I could hear Dad open the door, and then I heard Aunt Jessica say,

"Good evening, Gregory."

"Hello, Sister. I'm glad you could come over."

He didn't seem surprised to see her, which meant she had been invited. I went back to my room, which is directly over the living room. There is a register in the floor with a grille over it, so that in winter I get the benefit of the warm air rising from the room below. I never bother to close the register.

I could see down into the living room—that is, I had a good view of Aunt Jessica's ample lap and her feet in their sturdy black shoes, because Mother had seen to it that she sat in the morris chair. Mother was out of my range of vision altogether. I imagined that she was perched on the round piano stool, leaning her elbow on the back of the divan. Mother liked to get as far from the center of the room as possible during Family Discussions. It was soon apparent that this was going to be one of those.

Dad paced. He passed back and forth under my eye like a fish under a bridge. His left hand was plunged deeply into his coat pocket. His right hand was raised with the index finger pointed upward. I flinched every time it pointed toward me, although he had no idea I was peering down upon him.

"I asked you to come over, Jessica, for a particular reason," he began. "Do you have any idea why?"

I saw Aunt Jessica's finger tracing little patterns on her black crepe lap. "We haven't seen each other much lately," she answered.

"Jessica, you're evading my question!"

"Gregory, why don't you just come out with it!" Her voice was suddenly as sharp and thunderous as his. I pictured Mother cringing on the piano stool trying hard not to clap her hands over her ears.

"All right, then, I will! It has come to my attention that your business affairs are a mess—a terrible mess, as a matter of fact." The metal grille vibrated against my forehead. So someone at the bank had violated Aunt Jessica's confidence and had already spoken to Dad about her precarious situation. I was suddenly very angry. They had no right to do that.

"I see," she said quietly. "Who told you?"

"It doesn't matter how I found out. I could scarcely believe it, I'll tell you that! I wanted to withhold my judgment in the matter until I heard directly from you."

At that moment it occurred to me that perhaps Aunt Jessica would think *I* had told. I pressed my forehead against the metal grille and concentrated so hard I could feel my face wrinkle.

33

I didn't do it, Aunt Jessica. I promised you I wouldn't say a word and I didn't. I swear it.

"Well," she said, with a little sigh, "I'm very sorry that someone bothered you with that piece of news. It is none of your concern and I'm taking care of it quite well, thank you. You are not to worry."

"What do you mean I'm not to worry!" His usually smooth hair was suddenly disordered, his spectacles slid down his nose, his coat appeared to have folds and wrinkles that had not been there before. "I happen to feel responsible," he went on, turning away, "but you know very well that I warned you this might happen. I told you not to count on me to rescue you if you didn't succeed. Now, didn't I?"

"You did indeed. And I took you at your word. I have not asked for a cent from you and I don't intend to do so."

He whirled to face her. "But don't you see, I can't let you go under! Everyone in town knows you're my sister, and that you have no one to take care of you. What will people say if I allow you to go bankrupt?"

Aunt Jessica rose majestically to her feet. I could see her clearly then. Her round, florid face was darker than ever and her large bosom heaved under the tight black dress.

"Gregory, you're a pompous hypocrite! I will not be the object of your charity, goodness knows! I shall do all in my power to assure the citizens of Riverton that you had nothing to do with my misfortune. I can take care of myself!"

Dad stepped in front of her as she started toward the door. "Jessica, I don't think you have the right attitude about this. I'm not through talking."

"I am." She shoved him aside none too gently.

"Believe me, if I could get my hands on the person who aired my affairs to you, he would be sorry he ever opened his mouth!"

I couldn't bear the notion of her thinking I had been the stool pigeon. I jumped up with the intention of getting to her before she left. Then I heard her say, "Where's William?"

"He's upstairs studying his Sunday school lesson," Mother said. It was the first time she had spoken since the Discussion began. Her voice sounded thin and high.

"Humph!" said Aunt Jessica. They crowded through the doorway into the hall. I went back to the head of the stairs. My forehead tingled where it had pressed against the cold metal.

"William, come down here!" Aunt Jessica called, as though she knew perfectly well I was standing there in the dark.

The three of them were like statues with their faces tilted upward as I came downstairs. Mother looked anxious and imposed-upon. Dad glared at nothing in particular. Aunt Jessica's eyes searched my face. I met her look without flinching, for once in my life, and repeated silently what I had been thinking earlier. I didn't want her to suppose I had anything to do with it. I had enough enemies without making one of Aunt Jessica.

"What's the text?" she asked abruptly. I detected the ghost of a smile glimmering on her straight-line mouth.

" 'Enter ye in at the strait gate,' " I quoted heavily, rolling my eyes upward and pointing toward the ceiling. " 'For wide is the gate, and broad is the way, that leadeth to destruction, and many there be which go in threat: Because strait is the gate, and narrow is the way, which leadeth unto life, and few there be that find it.' "

She gave a little snort and fussed with her shawl. I had the feeling she was trying hard not to laugh.

"William, walk home with your aunt," Dad ordered.

"That isn't necessary," Aunt Jessica said. "But I will let him accompany me to the corner."

We went out together. As soon as we were out of earshot, I began my protestations. "Aunt Jessica, I swear I didn't—"

"William, do watch your language!"

"Cross my heart. I don't know how he found out."

"I believe you. It was Mr. Reavis at the bank—no doubt of it. So afraid he's going to lose his precious money. He'll get it some way, even if it means embarrassing Gregory. He *knows* Gregory can't stand to have anyone think his sister is destitute."

I was relieved to know that she still trusted me. We walked in silence for a few moments.

"Do you really have a way out of this mess?" I asked.

"It will come to me," she said.

I wished that I had the same confidence she did. I wished that I were rich.

We came to the corner. The streetlights gleamed on the gravel. "You may go back now," she told me. "I'll be quite all right. And, William—"

"Yes, ma'am?"

"Next time you listen through the register, don't press so hard against the grille. You have a checkerboard on your forehead. Good night."

3

RIVERTON HIGH SCHOOL is a two-story brick building situated on a corner two blocks from my house. It looks more like a federal post office than a school, with three dozen steps leading up to the front entrance, and globe lights on either side, like end-table lamps. The second bell rings at 8:45. I have learned that I can be precisely on time without even puffing if I leave home at 8:39. This always unnerves Miss Timothy, my English teacher, who likes students to be sitting in their desks ready to begin at 8:45. She has spoken to Mother, but the truth is, she has no case against me. I have never been tardy. I step inside room 109 just before the bell begins to ring.

On this particular Monday, because of all I had on my mind, I missed my timing. The bell was ringing, the door was closing in my face, and without thinking twice I stuck my foot in the narrowing wedge.

"Wait!" I shouted as the door crunched into my foot.

The door opened again, slowly, and I limped into the room. It wasn't easy to look sober and respectful with the class snickering. Miss Timothy's nostrils flared and her hard-line jaw clenched. I could see the little muscles moving under her ears—a dangerous sign.

"Good morning," I said.

She turned on her heel and marched to her desk, where the grade book lay open waiting for her to call the roll. "Shut the door, William, and take your seat!"

In making my way to the desk at the back of the room, I passed Paul Nisbett, who sat near the front so the teachers wouldn't forget what a nice guy he was. He didn't look up. He was writing something in ink. The paper was neat, without a sign of blot or smudge. I couldn't stand it. I jostled his elbow as I went by.

Lilly Fentrice was sitting across the aisle from me, to my right. After I sat down I looked over at her. Her eyes were fierce, just as they had been on Saturday when I had made her mad at the library.

"Meanie!" she mouthed.

I pretended not to know what she meant, but it didn't make me feel any too good to know that she had seen me bump Nisbett. A scheme had been taking shape in my mind all weekend, and Lilly was in it, although it was not yet clear to me what her role would be. One thing was certain, however, this was not a good time to make her mistrust me more than she already did.

"I'd like you to hand in the themes I asked you to write on the meaning of Easter," Miss Timothy said after calling the roll.

Themes! My stomach flipped. In all the excitement of the weekend I had completely forgotten the theme.

In such moments of panic either I am inspired or I draw a blank. In this case, I drew the blank. I fidgeted with my pencil and tried to think what I was

38

going to tell Miss Timothy.

I entertained the idea of conducting a Frantic Search, which consists of riffling through the pages of all my books, scattering bits of paper here and there, rumpling my hair, turning white, breaking out in a sweat, and finally saying, "Miss Timothy, I had it folded right here in my English book. I can't imagine what happened to it."

The problem is that the Frantic Search ploy is good only when used infrequently. I had used it scarcely two weeks before. I looked around. Every person in the room was busily folding themes lengthwise, as Miss Timothy required, and writing their names on the outside.

Miss Timothy seemed drawn toward me by negative vibrations. She moved down the aisle between two rows of desks, checking with sharp eyes. When she got to me she said, "William, where is your theme?"

I made myself look her in the eye, and perhaps that singular effort cleared my mind. At any rate, inspiration struck, and not a minute too soon.

"To be truthful, Miss Timothy, I couldn't bring myself to write a theme on that subject—The Meaning of Easter."

The room became very still.

"I see," said Miss Timothy. Her voice was chilly. "I suppose you think you are better than anyone else in the class, and therefore should not be required to do the same work?"

"Not at all," I said respectfully. "The problem is Constitutional—in this case it has to do with freedom of worship, or separation of church and state if you like."

Miss Timothy was sliding into a state of shock, but

39

she was not willing to yield.

"Easter is a Christian holy day," I went on, thankful for my training in declamation even if I hadn't won any medals. "It seems to me that to require a theme on this subject in a public school is a violation of the basic Constitutional rights of Jews, Moslems, and Buddhists."

Miss Timothy seemed to swell. Her eyes bulged.

"William Thomas, you are the most infuriating boy I have ever had the misfortune to teach!" Her long arm made a sweeping gesture that took in the whole classroom, the town, the world. "I have known every person here since they were infants. There *are* no Jews, Moslems, or Buddhists in this class—only Baptists, Methodists, Episcopalians, Presbyterians, Lutherans, Disciples of Christ, and Free Will Baptists!"

I inclined my head slightly, to give her the point. "That is true. The question is, would you have made the same assignment if, for instance, David Mandel had been in this class?"

When Miss Timothy blushed I knew I had hit pay dirt. David was in the other section of junior English. She did not want to believe that she was in a tough spot. On the other hand, thirty years of teaching had taught her to be cautious.

"Please pass your papers to the front," she said to the rest of the class. To me she added, "I'll discuss this with you when you come to see me this afternoon after school."

Staying after school was something I hadn't bargained for. Still, I was thankful for any sort of reprieve. Maybe I could convince Miss Timothy that I'd be happy to write a theme for her on almost any other subject.

While she gathered the papers I glanced at Lilly

once more. She looked thoughtful, as though she were turning over in her mind some new thing. I took that as a hopeful sign.

When the bell rang at the end of class, I swept my books off the desk and pushed through the jostling crowd to get to Bull.

"Say, Will!"

I turned. Paul Nisbett was at my elbow. "Yeah?"

"I liked what you said in class. I hadn't thought about it before, but you're exactly right—"

"Of course I'm right! I've got the whole U.S. Constitution to back me up." Who did he think he was, trying to impress me with that earnest good-old-boy look on his face? I took off after Bull, leaving Paul standing there looking foolish. The scheme I had been hatching all weekend was beginning to look good. It would need Lilly . . . innocent Lilly. I wasn't ready to tell Bull yet, but soon—very soon.

That afternoon when the final bell rang, I was the first to leave biology class. I lay in wait for Lilly outside the home economics classroom. When she came out, I fell in step beside her. She didn't like it.

"I want to know something," I said firmly, without any preliminaries. "Why were you giving me dirty looks in English class this morning?"

"You know why!"

"No, I don't. I think you owe me an explanation." I got in front of her, and she had to stop walking to look at me.

"I saw you bump Paul's elbow while he was writing." She faltered.

"You saw me what?"

She was silent. Her eyes focused on the buttons at the top of my shirt.

"Do you think I have it in for Nisbett or some-

41

thing? Well, I'm sorry if I've given that impression. Nisbett is a—fine fellow." I took her arm and steered her toward the door at the end of the hall.

"You're supposed to stay in for Miss Timothy," she said weakly.

"Don't worry about it. This is more important." We were next to the biology lab by that time. I stuck my head in the door, saw that no one was there, and pulled her inside. She began to get that white, scared look.

"I don't like for you to have a bad opinion of me," I said, looking down at her. I stuck my hands in my pockets and gazed out the narrow windows. Without looking at Lilly I could imagine the consternation in her heart as she tried to decide whether she pitied me, hated me, or what.

"I know I haven't exactly been the model student," I said after a minute of silence. "I've done a lot of things I'm not especially proud of. I'm tired of it. I want to change—really. But it isn't easy when people are suspicious of your every move."

I risked looking at her then, to see what sort of luck I was having. She was listening very hard. Her eyes showed the struggle that was going on in her. She wanted to give me the benefit of the doubt, but she also had a good memory. It would not be easy for her to forget all the teasing she had received from me.

"Look," I said. "I want to make it up to everyone —to you, to the teachers, even to Paul Nisbett."

"You don't have to make it up to me," she said.

"I think I do. As I said, your opinion of me is important."

"I don't see why—" she began. I gave her a soulful look and she forgot what she was going to say.

"I thought of volunteering my services to Miss

42

Lauderbach, to help her plan and carry out the Commencement program. I know with all the seniors she has a lot to worry about these next three weeks, and I thought maybe some student help from the junior class would be welcome."

"I think that's a fine idea! What did she say?"

I kicked the leg of a nearby desk with the side of my shoe. "I haven't talked to her yet. I don't think she'll give me a chance."

"Why on earth not?"

I sighed. "You've been in all of my classes for most of my school career, Lilly. Miss Lauderbach has put up with my—shall we say—mischief until I'm sure she suspects something every time I look at her straight. Or crooked. I don't know how to convince her that this time I'm on the level."

"Well, just tell her the same thing you've told me. Miss Lauderbach is a very understanding person."

I shook my head. "I don't think it will work unless—"

"Unless what?"

"Lilly, would you be willing to go with me? Maybe if we both offered our services, Miss Lauderbach would . . . ah . . . be more inclined to accept."

She shook her head, but it seemed more a device to clear her brain than anything else. "I'll have to think about it."

"O.K. I'll wait. And, Lilly—"

She looked up at me. Her eyes were large, rather fine-looking eyes, actually. I forgot what I had intended to say, but it didn't matter. She turned deep red and fled. I stood there a minute, sorting out my feelings, and then turned and went upstairs to my meeting with Miss Timothy and a discussion of the Constitution.

4

MISS TIMOTHY did not go so far as to admit she was wrong, but she did give me a two-day reprieve on the theme and let me choose my own topic. I felt that I had achieved my goal—more time.

Aunt Jessica expected me to report for work no later than three fifteen on school days, but she didn't say anything about my being late this time. I suppose it had something to do with the fact that I might be working for nothing, and under those circumstances she couldn't be too severe. I decided not to tell her I had succeeded in removing Riverton High one notch farther from the established religious community. Although she is Baptist and believes in separation of church and state more than most, I knew she would question my motives. I wasn't sure they would bear questioning.

She was sitting at her desk, poring over papers when I came in. Her spectacles had slid to the end of her nose. "Good afternoon, William."

"Hullo." I hung my cap on the coatrack at the back of the store. "Anything new?"

"No."

The word had a finality about it that did not invite further questions. But my curiosity is not easily satisfied. I went over and sat chummily on the edge of the desk.

"William, kindly get off!"

I jumped up hastily. "Yes, ma'am. What would you like me to do first?"

"A number of people have returned books to the library today. I've been much too busy to card and shelve them."

"I'll get right on it." I started upstairs. "Uh . . . you say business has been pretty good today?"

I must have sounded too eager. She looked at me as I hung over the banister, as though she couldn't decide whether to laugh or to weep.

"My dear boy, I didn't say that at all! I said *I* had been busy." It was the second time in three minutes that she had put me in my place. I went upstairs.

I kept thinking about Lilly Fentrice and began to feel restless. I did not want her to occupy my thoughts more than was necessary. She was part of my plan and that was all.

I reached under the desk and pulled out the copy of *What Every Young Boy Should Know*. Aunt Jessica was not supposed to censor reading matter, but she had her ways. She kept "questionable" literature in a cubbyhole under the desk. I wasn't allowed to check out those books, nor to let anyone else do so. Aunt Jessica alone made those decisions. Naturally, I had read them all. This particular one was full of intriguing information. It was the best diversion the Riverton Public Library offered. However, this time it did nothing for me. I was in a low mood.

The library was still and gloomy, even with the lights on. I got up and went to the front windows and leaned my forehead against one grimy pane. Down in the street the automobiles moved along at a snail's pace, their flat black tops looking like the hats of solemn old men. There were some horses pulling farm wagons, and a few people on the sidewalks and street corners. It was a placid, dull scene. Riverton, North Carolina. What if I ended up like G.C., living at home and working every day at the bookstore?

I balled up my fist and hit the window frame to make myself quit thinking about it. The future looked boring, bleak, and as gloomy as this dusty-smelling library. People like Paul Nisbett got what *I* wanted without half trying—without even wishing for it. The more they had, and the less they needed, the more they got. It was unfair. I hit the frame again and felt a kind of relief in the throb of bruised knuckles.

I heard the stairs creaking, so I pulled a book or two from a nearby shelf and pretended to be putting them back in place. It wouldn't do for Aunt Jessica to catch me daydreaming.

The head that appeared at the top of the stairs was not hers but Mrs. Benson's.

"Hello, William," she said pleasantly. She didn't ask a lot of silly questions about school, but set about looking through the books. I went back to the desk. But instead of shelving the books that were piled on the cart, I studied her. The shadow of an idea was taking shape in the back of my mind and it had something to do with Mrs. Benson, although I was not certain what.

This lady and my aunt were the closest of friends. You would think that any intimate of Aunt Jessica's would have to be like her—large and forceful. But Mrs. Benson was a small gray person, younger than Aunt Jessica. Her hair was soft and fluffed, her eyes blue-gray like the ocean on a cloudy day. Her skin was pale, and she wore colorless clothes. Alongside her renowned husband, the aforementioned Dr. Benson with whom Aunt Jessica had tangled in town meeting, she almost seemed to disappear.

I knew that Aunt Jessica called on Mrs. Benson at their Hildebrande Avenue mansion, but they did not move in the same social circles. Mrs. Benson, as the wife of an internationally famous surgeon and a High Church Episcopalian, was obliged to entertain frequently. She gave bridge parties and teas and large dinners—or so I understood. My family was not invited to these functions. Aunt Jessica, past president of the Woman's Christian Temperance Union, was against card-playing, strong drink, smoking, dancing, and meaningless conversation. But their friendship was solid. Mrs. Benson called her "Jess" and she called Mrs. Benson "Kate." The library was their common faith. They were obsessed with the value of books and the worth of words, and it was no secret in town that when Dr. Benson had opposed the public tax for the library, Mrs. Benson had been one of its staunchest advocates.

Dr. Benson, you must know, was Riverton's claim to Fame. Born on Third Street, he had gone North to medical school in his youth and had become one of the nation's most sought-after surgeons. His former patients had included admirals, statesmen, generals, and even a famous baseball player. He had maintained a home in Riverton to which he returned from time to time for brief visits, but not until he retired did he come back to live. He had married late in life. Mrs. Benson was about my mother's age. Dr. Benson was old enough to be my grandfather.

Mrs. Benson turned toward me suddenly and caught me staring at her. "Is something the matter, William?"

"N-no. Of course not. I was wondering whether you had—ah—read this book yet. It's a new one. Just came in a couple of days ago." I grabbed up a book that was lying on the desk without really looking at it, thinking that it was a new novel I had noticed earlier.

"Why, no, I don't think so." She came over and started to take the book from my hand. That's when I took a good look at the title.

And almost had a stroke. It was *What Every Young Boy Should Know.* Mrs. Benson's fingers closed upon thin air. I was already stuffing the book under the desk.

My face burned. "I—uh—just remembered that someone has a request in for that book. Sorry." I couldn't look her in the eye.

"Well, perhaps you have another suggestion." The kindness in her voice flustered me more than ever. In desperation my eyes swept over the books on the cart. There was a recent Zane Grey—*To the Last Man.* I handed it to her.

"Thank you," she said, "and I'll just keep looking on the shelves over here. Once in a while I come upon one I've missed."

She turned away and I drew a shaky breath and wiped my perspiring forehead. One thing for sure, she wasn't going to catch me staring at her any more that day!

The stairs squeaked again, this time under a much heavier tread. I set to work in double time, knowing without looking that it was Aunt Jessica.

The two of them sat down at one of the reading

48

tables and began chatting. When Mrs. Benson came, Aunt Jessica broke her own rules about talking in the library. No one, including me, had the courage to call her attention to that inconsistency.

Without anything else to claim my attention I finished shelving the books in record time, putting away the last of the Q's and the W's before ten minutes were up. I could hear the ladies' voices murmuring like quiet bees. Then Aunt Jessica's voice suddenly grew louder.

"Kate—you don't mean it! How could he do such a thing to you, of all people?"

I froze. It didn't seem the time to make myself visible.

"Please don't be upset, Jess. It will all work out. I'm sure of it."

"The idea!" Aunt Jessica snorted. I heard her hand slap the table.

"If you can wait just a little longer—"

"I can wait as long as is necessary," Aunt Jessica said with great firmness. "You needn't worry about that. It's *you* I'm concerned about."

"I can take care of myself." The words were brave, but Mrs. Benson's tone was uncertain.

I took a couple of books off the shelf and dropped them on the floor. I made a lot of fuss getting them back into place. When the voices became hushed again, I made my appearance.

"I'm through," I said, looking as blank as I could. "I'll go stay in the store if you want me to."

"Yes, of course." Aunt Jessica seemed preoccupied. "Did you speak to Mrs. Benson?"

"Yes, ma'am." I ducked my head and avoided Mrs. Benson's eyes.

Downstairs I wandered around among the coun-

49

ters. The fragment of conversation I had heard bothered me. Someone was harassing quiet little Mrs. Benson. Quiet, rich little Mrs. Benson—

The idea that had been floating half-formed in my mind suddenly came to life, full-blown. Rich little Mrs. Benson. Why, of course! Dr. Benson was the richest man in Riverton—maybe the richest in the whole state. Mrs. Benson was Aunt Jessica's best friend. All my aunt had to do was to swallow her pride and ask—

But that was no small thing. Asking her to swallow her pride was in the same vein as asking a normal person to eat a whole elephant. She had an enormous amount of pride. It was her most plenteous commodity. The problem was how to make her see that it was more sensible to borrow the money from her friend than to let the town banker bludgeon her pride.

I was struggling with the problem when they came downstairs. They exchanged a few words more. Then Mrs. Benson called good-by to me and went out.

I studied Aunt Jessica's face to judge what sort of mood she was in. She was none too happy, that was certain. Still, there was no time to waste beating around the bush. I plunged in.

"I have an idea how you can settle your financial problem without Dad's help or the bank's."

She gave me one of her searching looks. "Is it honest?"

"Of course it's honest! Do you think I'd have the nerve to suggest something dishonest to you?"

Aunt Jessica laughed—a solid, hearty, unexpected jolly laugh. My spirits lifted.

"All right," she said, "what is it?"

I told her.

And watched the laughter that had crinkled her

50

eyes fade and disappear. Her face became stern again.

"No. Absolutely not."

I shook my head. "I don't understand you. This woman is your best friend. She would do anything for you. You would do anything for *her*. God knows—"

"William!"

"Anyone knows that if she were in the same circumstances, you would give her the shirt off your ba—I mean, you would share your last penny with her. You've got to quit being so proud, Aunt Jessica. Give someone a chance to do something for you once in a while!"

I was really carried away by that time, striding up and down, waving my arms. For once I knew I was right. It was a great idea. If I spoke with enough conviction, she would be persuaded.

"William, that's enough."

Aunt Jessica's voice has a way of stabbing through bubbles and dreams. They pop and dwindle away like the Wicked Witch of the West. It was very quiet in the store. She looked at the watch pinned on her ample bosom.

"It's time to close up. Go upstairs and turn off the lights in the library, please."

I was angry and didn't care if she knew it. I stamped up the stairs, half expecting her to shout a reprimand. I had already made up my mind to ignore her if she did, but she didn't give me the satisfaction. That's the trouble with Aunt Jessica. No matter how fast I go, her mind is already three jumps ahead. In some ways it is very discouraging.

I pulled down the shades and switched off the overhead lights. At the desk I was about to switch off the lamp when my eye fell upon a book card that had not been put in the file. "Grey, Zane. *To the Last Man.*" Beside the date was Mrs. Benson's signature. Her signature also appeared by an earlier date.

She had already read the book.

Then I realized what she had done. She had taken the book to relieve my embarrassment. Just thinking about it made my face grow hot again. I switched off the light viciously and clattered back downstairs.

5

I HAVE LONG SINCE learned that it is better to do a dreaded task in the heat of impulse than to sit around thinking about it too long. On Tuesday, as soon as I got to the bookstore, I asked Aunt Jessica for the afternoon off.

"The entire afternoon? What have you done?"

"Nothing. It's just that I have some important business to attend to. It won't wait."

Aunt Jessica studied me. At last she said, "Very well. Tuesdays aren't so busy anyway."

"Thanks! You won't regret it." I started out, but before I had gotten to the door she called me.

"William!"

"Yes, Aunt Jessica?"

"I *hope* I won't regret it."

I ducked my head and said something dumb. It was a relief to get out on the sidewalk. I still wasn't absolutely sure she couldn't read minds.

On the way to Hildebrande Avenue I carefully reviewed the reasons for doing what I was about to do. They were all sensible—unshakable. Why did I feel uneasy?

One look at Dr. Benson's mansion answered my question. Although I had passed it hundreds of times on my way home in the afternoon, somehow it had never seemed so imposing as it did now. I would have to go inside the ironwork fence and along the winding flagstone walkway, up to the carved front door.

The lawn, green and manicured, stretched away to some remote point beyond my range of vision. Near the house was a flower garden with trellises and stone benches and a marble fountain that ran continually. The fountain was the statue of a boy with no clothes on. He held up a fish from whose mouth the water squirted up and out. His gaze was vacant and unconcerned. I averted my eyes.

Suddenly I wanted nothing quite so much as to be back in Brassey's Book Nook among the boxes of stationery and playing cards. All my planning and rationalizing dwindled away to a raisin-sized wad of confused notions. Aunt Jessica was right. Asking Mrs. Benson for money was the wrong thing to do.

Fate has a peculiar way of taking charge at such critical moments. Just when I had decided to forget the whole thing, a long gray Buick with Mrs. Benson in the back seat pulled up to the curb in front of the gate. A chauffeur leaped from the automobile to open the gate. Mrs. Benson rapped upon the window with the handle of her umbrella and beckoned to me.

I went over and she rolled the window down.

"Good afternoon, William! What a pleasure to see you."

"Thank you," I said. "I was just walking by."

"Oh, I see. I saw you standing by the gate and I . . . I thought perhaps you had come to call." She sounded disappointed.

"I . . . uh . . . have always been interested in . . . flowers." I gestured toward her garden. "I always like to look when I pass this way."

Mrs. Benson beamed. "Then you shall come in and see them up close! Richard, drive the car in and let us off by the garden if you please." And she proceeded to move over in the seat and make room for me.

What should I do? You don't keep a lady waiting—Mother and Aunt Jessica have certainly drilled that into me. I opened the car door and got in, although I could read the chauffeur's disapproval as clearly as though it had been written in silver letters on the back of his head.

The inside of the Buick was luxurious beyond imagining. I tried not to stare as Richard drove through the gate, got out once more to shut it behind us, and then drove us up the gravel driveway to the garden.

Mrs. Benson bubbled. "You know, I never would have thought that you were a flower lover. Most young men don't have time for such."

I could feel myself blushing. For one thing, I wasn't used to being called a young man. For another, I hardly knew a pansy from a petunia.

"Well," I said, truthfully enough, "it's not the sort of thing a guy talks about to his friends, if you know what I mean."

"Of course. I understand perfectly."

Richard stopped the automobile once more and opened the door for Mrs. Benson. I got out quickly on the other side. I certainly didn't want him opening the door for me!

"Shall I wait, madam?"

"No, Richard. We'll walk up to the house when we're through looking at the flowers. You might tell Mrs. Hampton to fix us something to drink. We'll be in directly."

I suppressed a sigh and looked back at the iron

gate, which seemed ever so firm and strong. Was it locked? Would I be able to leave when I was ready?

"Now, these," said Mrs. Benson happily, pointing with her furled umbrella, "are some cacti I brought from home. I wasn't at all sure that they would grow here, but they survive if I take them up in winter. You know, the flowers here are so different from the varieties we had in California."

"You're from California?"

"Yes. I grew up there."

"Gee!" I said. "Have you ever been to Hollywood?"

Mrs. Benson laughed. "Once. Once was enough."

I wanted to ask whether she had seen Theda Bara, or John Barrymore, or Tom Mix, but it was the flowers she was interested in. I followed her through the little winding pathways of the garden while she pointed out all manner of flowers and told me the names, which I promptly forgot. When we walked by the fountain I looked the other way. It was embarrassing being around that naked boy with a lady.

"Very well," she said, looking up at last. "I think it's time for some refreshment. Come along." She led the way to the porch and twisted the bell. The door opened instantly and a butler stood there holding it for us. His nose was lifted and his eyes focused on something beyond me.

"Madam," he said. It was a kind of greeting, a question, and a statement all in one.

"Hastings, William and I will be in the front parlor. Please have Fan bring in the refreshments right away."

"Veddy good, madam." He inclined his head slightly and went away, still not soiling his gaze by looking at me. I stole a look at my scuffed brown shoes, the argyle knee socks with the hole just above my shoe top, and the pants that clung loosely just below the knee with sagging knit that bagged outward. I did not fit in with the elegant surroundings.

But Mrs. Benson didn't seem to notice. We went into the front parlor, and she indicated that I should sit in a rose satin chair. I almost forgot and sat before she did, but remembered just as I was about to bend my knees. I don't think she saw.

"This is a real pleasure," she said to me. "You know, I don't often get to see young people anymore, and I miss it dreadfully. I used to teach school, before I married Dr. Benson. I dearly loved being with all my boys and girls."

"Oh, well," I said, "at least now you don't have to put up with bad manners and laziness."

Mrs. Benson seemed surprised that I should say such a thing. "But they were all lovely!"

The maid came in just then with a tray of goodies and Mrs. Benson busied herself with seeing that it was arranged properly and all. I decided she must not have taught in a place like Riverton High School, if all her "boys and girls" were lovely. Naturally it would be a ritzy place for rich kids, and they wouldn't be lazy or ignorant.

The drink was pink lemonade. We had some thin little cookies that didn't have much taste. I much preferred Mother's fat tea cakes for eating purposes, but of course they wouldn't look too elegant on a silver tray.

Suddenly Mrs. Benson set down her glass and looked at me.

"I thought you worked for Jess in the afternoons!"

"Yes, ma'am."

"Oh, dear!" She looked quite distressed. "I'll bet

anything you were on your way to work, and you were too polite to tell me. How terrible of me! You really shouldn't let a lonely old woman keep you from doing your duty."

"Oh, it's all right. Aunt Jessica gave me the afternoon off."

"I see." But she didn't. I could see the puzzlement in her eyes. Fate again. It was like Opportunity stood there holding the door wide open. I wasn't even required to knock.

"Actually," I said, setting my glass carefully on the tray, "Aunt Jessica isn't . . . well, I don't know how to say it."

"She's well, isn't she?"

"Oh, yes. The problem is—business isn't too good just now. I'm . . . never sure whether she'll be able to pay my wages at the end of the week."

Mrs. Benson's eyes grew round. "What? Is that true?"

I nodded. "Or—maybe I should say business is moderately good. If it weren't for the fact that she was in arrears in her payments on the loan from the bank, I think she could manage quite well."

Mrs. Benson took it too hard. I didn't expect her to turn white and press her fine hands to her bosom like some movie heroine. "Oh, William," she said, "why didn't she tell me?"

"You know Aunt Jessica. I only found out by accident myself. She has too much pride to ask for *help.*" I purposely came down hard on the last word.

"Terrible. Just terrible," Mrs. Benson muttered over and over. She seemed to have forgotten I was there. I ate another tasteless cookie and waited for her to calm down.

"What she must *think* of me!" Mrs. Benson stood up and began to pace. I stood up too, because you aren't supposed to remain seated when a lady is walking around.

"You didn't have any way of knowing she was in trouble if she didn't tell you," I said reasonably. "Aunt Jessica wouldn't impose on a friendship."

Instead of comforting her, my words seemed to bring on more agitation.

"That is so true," Mrs. Benson said sorrowfully. "If only some of the rest of us had her integrity!"

I thought she was talking about me and began to feel uncomfortable. Thank goodness I hadn't come right out and asked her for the money. At least this way I had only shared Aunt Jessica's plight with her best friend. If Mrs. Benson didn't want to do anything about it, then that was her business. And if she didn't do anything about it, she was no kind of friend to have.

"I should go now," I said, eyeing the ormulu clock on the carved white mantel.

Mrs. Benson collected herself then and tried to get me to sit down and have more lemonade and cookies, but she was rather halfhearted about it. When I refused—politely, of course—she rang for the butler to show me to the door.

"Thank you, William, for coming to visit, and for— for letting me know Jess's true situation."

"Thank *you*, for the cookies and all. And—I'd appreciate it if you wouldn't tell Aunt Jessica."

I looked sideways at the butler.

"Of course," said Mrs. Benson. "Don't worry."

She sounded as though she were trying to convince herself. It was all very strange. I followed the butler's rigid spine to the front door.

"Thank you," I said when he opened it for me and stood aside.

He merely inclined his head and closed his eyes in a bored way. I went out. For not much I would have poked him in the ribs just to get him to look at me.

6

I HEARD THE TOWN CLOCK strike the half hour. Four thirty was too early to go home. Maybe Aunt Jessica would welcome my presence, especially since she wasn't expecting me. I headed downtown.

On an impulse I stopped in at Crenshaw's Grocery. Bull was between deliveries. He was surprised to see me.

"What're you doing here? Get fired?"

"You'd like that, wouldn't you?" I said.

"Naw—at least not until you pay me back the two bucks you owe me."

"Do I owe you *that* much?"

"Sure do. I got it written down."

"Whew! I didn't know it was that much."

"I'll take it in quarters," Bull said, grinning at me as he loaded a box with groceries. "That's how it left me—in quarters."

I inhaled the atmosphere of overripe bananas, smoked meat, and sweet cakes and watched him fitting the grocery items neatly into the box. He was good at it. Two bucks. How had I managed to let that slip up on me?

"I dropped by to tell you a couple of things. Maybe I could go along when you make the delivery."

"Sure. Be ready in a second."

Mr. Crenshaw came out of the back room. He frowned slightly when he saw me.

"Bull, take those groceries and come straight back here. There's plenty to do."

"Yes, sir." Bull was a lot more amiable about it than I would have been. We started out the back door to the alley where Bull kept his bicycle.

"And mind you don't take all afternoon!" Mr. Crenshaw called after us.

Bull ignored him. He set the box of groceries in the large square wicker basket fastened to the handlebars. "What's on your mind? And why aren't you working?"

I told him I had the afternoon off because business was slow. No need to say I had asked for it—too much explaining. Bull pedaled slowly. I jogged along beside him.

"Tomorrow," I panted, "is the crucial day."

"What do you mean?"

"Tomorrow . . . we vie . . . for Lilly Fentrice's favor."

"We do *what?*" Bull stopped the bike and I almost collided with him.

"You're going to ask to walk her home. Then I'm going to come along and ask to walk her home. And we will appear to argue about it."

Bull's forehead was crimped in a hundred wrinkles. "I don't get it. What's that for?"

"She will be indispensable to us during the next couple of weeks. We want her on our side—absolutely loyal. What could make a girl more loyal than to know a guy—two guys—are fighting for her attention? Especially when nobody else is paying her any mind."

62

I could tell he hadn't arrived at that point in his thinking, but after a second or two his face cleared. He shrugged and started pedaling again. "O.K. If you say so, I guess I can do that. But I have to work tomorrow. Mr. Crenshaw won't like me coming in late."

"Then tell him something came up at school. They always give you time off for school stuff."

"I don't get paid for time I don't work."

"Don't *worry* about it. If you lose a lot, I'll make it up to you."

He gave me a look and I was reminded that I was already in debt to him.

"It won't matter," I said. "It isn't going to take that much time to walk Lilly home. It's right on your way to work. Besides, I have to work too."

"I take it," said Bull, "that you have come up with something to enliven the Commencement exercises?"

"I think you could say that."

"What's Lilly got to do with it?"

"That will come to light. The important thing is for her to believe in us."

Bull looked at me like I was some kind of loony, but I didn't let it bother me. He would catch on sooner or later. I turned to go back the way we had come. "Just don't forget tomorrow after school," I said.

I watched him pedal off up Langley Street shaking his head. Good old Bull! His not to reason why—

The town clock was striking five when I bounced into Brassey's Book Nook. Several late customers were browsing among the new books. Aunt Jessica was surprised to see me.

"What are you doing here?" Her voice echoed all

63

over the store. The customers looked up curiously. I nodded at them.

"Just thought you might need me for something." I stuffed my hands in my pockets.

She lowered her voice. "What have you been up to?"

"Good works," I said piously. "I daresay you would be proud of me." I could actually look her in the eye, because for once she was going to benefit directly from my brainwork. "Aunt Jessica, you always reserve the right to keep your business affairs to yourself—and I respect that. I hope you will allow me the same."

She was startled, but after a moment she said, "Very well. Excuse my nosiness. But frankly, I worry sometimes about your too-active imagination. I shouldn't want you to get into serious trouble because of it."

"Don't worry—everything is going to be *fine!*" I smiled broadly, which rather than comforting her seemed to make her more uneasy than ever. It was hard for me not to tell her my afternoon's adventure, but I managed to keep it to myself.

Seconds after the last bell rang Wednesday afternoon, Bull and I were out on the sidewalk in front of the school. All day I had been doing what I thought was an admirable job of reforming my in-school behavior. Even Bull confessed to being amazed.

"Miss Timothy thinks you're sick," he said. "Or that you're having some terrible trouble at home that has dampened your spirits. I heard her tell Mr. Bailey this morning."

"Let her think it!" I laughed. "There's more to come—and it's going to pay off the night of Commencement exercises if we play our cards right. But our plans depend on Lilly. Don't forget that."

"I like the way you say 'our plans,'" Bull said. "I don't recall straining my brain over any plans. Matter of fact, I don't know what you're going to do. Seems as though the least you could do would be to fill me in, as long as I'm risking life and limb."

He shoved his hands into his pockets and worriedly scrutinized the crowds of students pouring out of the school. He looked nervous. I wasn't used to seeing Bull like that.

"Look," I said. "Trust me. But if you don't think you can bring this off in a convincing manner—"

"Sure I can! What do you think I am—a slouch or something? It's not all that hard. We both pretend we're stuck on her—right? And then we argue over who's going to walk her home and you win—right?"

I nodded. He was frowning a lot. I began to wish we had a different strategy, but it was too late to change. I spotted Lilly coming out of the basement entrance.

"O.K. Here she comes. Get ready!" I poked him in the ribs and he stiffened to attention. "And for Pete's sake, relax!"

Lilly came along the walk hauling a huge pile of books. I could read her face. She had seen me and had made up her mind to pretend she hadn't. Her eyes wandered somewhere to the right. I poked Bull again and he stepped directly in front of her. She had to come to a sudden halt to keep from running into him.

"If you don't mind, I'd like to get by," she said, trying to step around him.

"Hello-Lilly-on-your-way-home?"

I smothered a groan. Bull had rehearsed his line so

65

much that it came out like a telegram.

"I beg your pardon?"

He took a deep breath and tried again. There was a fine film of moisture on his forehead. "I said, were you on your way home? I'd like to walk with you."

"Yes, of course I'm on my way home. . . ." There was something unfinished about the way she said it, as though maybe she didn't want Bull to walk home with her. I had expected that. It was my cue.

"Hello, Lilly." I smiled and made my voice tender. I reached for her books. "How about letting me carry these for you?"

She bit her lip and frowned. "That's all right. I can carry them myself."

I was stronger, and she didn't put up much resistance.

"Say!" said Bull. "*I* asked Lilly first! What's the big idea, horning in like that?"

"Maybe you didn't do it right," I said.

"There wasn't anything wrong with the way I did it!"

I shrugged. Bull was playing his part very well. "Why don't we let Lilly decide?"

We both turned to her. It was almost more than she could handle. Probably it was the first time in her life she had had even one boy ask to walk with her, much less two. She made a helpless little gesture with her hands.

"I d-don't care. I wasn't planning to walk with anyone. I'm going home. If you walk along, that's up to you." She turned on her heel and started away. That wasn't exactly the way I had planned it. One thing was becoming clear—Lilly didn't know anything about flirting. Bull looked at me and I looked at him. Obviously he expected me to do something.

"Hey! I've got your books," I said, hastening to catch up with her.

"I never asked you to carry my books. Give them back."

"No, that's not what I meant." I held them away from her reaching arms. "I mean, how can you go off and leave me?"

By this time Bull had caught up and there we were, the three of us, hogging the sidewalk, Bull on one side of Lilly and me on the other. Bull, not to be outclassed, snatched a couple of books from the pile when I wasn't watching. Lilly kept looking around to see if anyone was noticing. She would have been much happier if she had been invisible. Bull and I were enjoying ourselves with a kind of friendly rivalry to see who could get Lilly's attention. I'll have to hand it to Bull. He'd been around me so long he could almost read my mind. For instance, I was about to make the big pitch when he said, "Say, why do you have to go home right this minute, Lilly? We could go over to Bainbridge's and have a Coke. Too bad old Will here has to go to work!"

"What do you mean? *You're* the one has to go to work. *I* don't have to go to work until I want to!"

"Ha! That tough old aunt of yours won't put up with your coming in late every afternoon. You told me so yourself."

"She will now," I said stubbornly. "We have an arrangement. And I'll thank you not to cast aspersions on my lady relatives!"

"Oh, for heaven's sake!" Lilly said, laying a hand on each of our arms. "It's not worth fighting about. You can *both* take me to Bainbridge's."

So we all three ended up in Bainbridge's Drugstore, sitting at one of those little bitty round black

67

tables, bumping knees. The black-and-white square tiles made me feel like a pawn on a chessboard. This certainly was not how I had intended the game to go. I thought Bull was overdoing it, but how could I let him know? Lilly's books were piled on the floor at my feet. There were lots of other kids from school, since Bainbridge's is a favorite afternoon stopping place for the Riverton crowd. Whether it was true or not, I felt their eyes upon us. Lilly seemed to feel it too. Her face was perpetually red.

"O.K., Bull, since you're such a gentleman, go buy our Cokes." I gave him my last dollar with a flourish.

"What do you mean, buy our Cokes! I—"

I gave him a look that stopped him in the middle of his protest, and he went to the soda fountain for the drinks, grumbling all the way. Lilly pushed her hair back nervously. She wouldn't look at me.

"I hope you've been thinking about what I said Monday," I began.

"You mean . . . about volunteering with you to help with the Commencement program?" Her eyes focused on her fingernails, which were short and chewed-looking.

"Yes. I still haven't talked to Miss Lauderbach. I was waiting for you to decide." I looked at *my* fingernails, which were too long and dirty. Lilly took a deep breath, like a diver who is about to plunge into a tank of cold water.

"All right," she said. "I'll go with you to talk to Miss Lauderbach."

Home Free! I almost jumped up and yelled, but I didn't. "That's great! We can—"

"But so help me, Will Thomas, if you're up to one of your tricks, I promise you will live to regret the day you ever thought of it!"

68

Her voice was so firm and her gaze so piercing that I found myself casting about for something to say. I blinked and swallowed. "Why are you so suspicious? I am a changed man, Lilly. That's the truth."

"I'd like to believe that," she said softly, and her eyes looked straight into mine. Something hot exploded in my chest and flowed down my arms and legs. Fortunately Bull came back to the table just then clutching three Cokes and my change in his stubby hands. The diversion gave me time to collect my wits and to remember why we were there. Mustn't forget that. Ever.

"You look funny," Bull told me when he was seated.

"I was born that way."

"No—I mean you look kind of sick."

"You're just trying to get rid of me." But I avoided Bull's eyes. I wasn't feeling any too good—that was the truth—but I couldn't understand why. I should have been feeling great. I had gotten what I wanted.

"Lilly's going to help me with a project." I tried to weight the words with meaning so he would know our efforts had paid off.

Bull put his elbows on the tiny table and leaned in until our three heads were practically touching. "Tell me about it," he said, looking from one to the other, alternately blinking his eyes and rubbing his nose. It was very irritating.

"Will says he wants to be more responsible and helpful," Lilly said.

"Does he now?"

"He has asked me to go with him to Miss Lauderbach, to volunteer our services in planning the Commencement program."

"I see." Bull sucked hard at his straw and the drink

disappeared rapidly before our eyes. "And you're going to do it?"

"Why, yes, I think so."

"Well," he said, "I guess that's that."

"Yes," I said slowly. "I guess it is."

"And I have to be going home." Lilly stood up. I jumped up too. My foot nudged the pile at my feet. The books fell over noisily, sliding and spreading themselves out on the checkered floor.

"Bull, you're so clumsy!" I said loudly. "Don't just stand there. Pick up the lady's books!"

As soon as I said the words, I was sorry. An expression I had never seen came into Bull's eyes. Without a word he bent over and picked up the books.

"Come on, Lilly," he said, not looking at me. "I'll walk you home."

She followed him out of the drugstore, with her hands sort of hanging off the ends of her arms as though she didn't quite know what to do. I followed her, trying to ignore the snickers and giggles from the tables we passed.

Out on the sidewalk I tried to stop Bull. "It was just a joke. Come on. Don't take it so seriously!"

"Some joke! Come on, Lilly."

"No. Give me my books."

"But—"

"Give them to me. I'm going home alone. Both of you go to your jobs, where you belong."

She took the books in her frail-looking arms and marched away without so much as a backward glance.

"Well," I began, when she had turned the corner and was out of sight, "I guess—"

But Bull was walking away too. I was left standing like a dumbbell on the sidewalk in front of Bainbridge's.

70

7

I STAYED AT WORK an extra thirty minutes that afternoon to make up for being late, but Aunt Jessica wasn't impressed. She took it for granted that staying late was the only right thing for me to do.

When I came out of the store the sky had begun to cloud over and a strong breeze had sprung up. I hunched my shoulders against the wind and walked along looking at the cracks in the sidewalk, thinking about what had happened in Bainbridge's and the look Bull had given me. The memory of that look made me cross the street and go down by Crenshaw's Grocery. The light was still on, but when I tried the front door it was locked. Bull had already gone home. The wind blew harder, swirling the dust in the street and plastering scraps of paper against the sides of buildings.

Bull lived on the west end of Third Street, a good four blocks beyond our house. I wasn't too crazy about the idea of going down there. Many of the people who lived in that neighborhood were what my mother called hand-to-mouth. The men mostly worked at the Archimedes Lumber Mill. There was talk of drinking and wife-beating after dark. The kids from those families often came to school in the same

71

clothes several days in a row. They slept a lot in class too.

Bull's family wasn't like that. His father was a butcher and his mother did dress alterations at Bremer's Department Store. Bull had lots of brothers and sisters. I suppose the fact that there were so many of them had something to do with their staying where they were instead of moving to a different part of town.

The town clock struck the quarter hour. Except for where the sun was going down, the sky was almost completely overcast. I wouldn't let myself think anymore—just struck out for Bull's house.

There were no sidewalks or gutters along Third, and no paving. Many of the houses stood up high on brick pillars. By looking under them you could see all the way to back fences. Every place I passed sent forth smells of cabbage boiling and pork or fish frying.

The street ended abruptly at a wide drainage ditch. Across the ditch bank and the vacant field beyond, the Archimedes Lumber Mill loomed, blocking the sunset colors from view. Third Street could have used some color.

The front door to the Clammetts' house stood open, and through the screen I could see into the narrow hallway. A muddle of family voices and rattling dishes came floating out to me from the kitchen at the back of the house. A sudden gust of wind whistled around the side of the porch, mixing the smell of rain with the hot grease and cabbage. I knocked loudly on the frame of the screen door.

After what seemed a long time, Bull's older sister Dolores appeared. She was bookkeeper at Marcus' Hardware store. She peered through the screen at me and her eyes widened.

"For heaven's sake!" she exclaimed. "What are *you* doing here?"

"I—I need to see Bull. Could he come out here?"

"We're eating supper."

I stood on one foot, then on the other. "I know. I'm sorry—but it just won't wait." Another gust of wind blew across the porch and I shivered.

"Wait a minute," she said. "I'll go get him." She turned away, then came back, laying a hand upon the screen. "Has—is G.C. all right?"

I wasn't sure I had understood. "I beg your pardon?"

"Is G.C. all right?"

"Well, I suppose so. I haven't seen him today. You've probably seen him since I have. Why? Did he get sick at work or something?"

"No. I just—I'll go get Bull."

I sat down on the top step and leaned my chin on my hands, puzzling over Dolores' question. The wind was definitely chilly now. The light was fading fast. Soon it would be dark. There weren't any street-lights at this end of town. I thought about the drinking and wife-beating. I didn't want to be on Third Street when it started.

The screen door hinges squeaked as Bull came out on the porch. He stood looking down at me, his clothes reeking of fried fish, his face a mask.

"Hi!" I said, forcing a grin.

"Did you want me for something?"

The grin slid away. I got up and faced him. "Bull, I did a stupid thing this afternoon, and I'm sorry it embarrassed you."

Bull shrugged. "Don't worry about it. Is that all you wanted?"

"Yeah, I guess so." But it seemed unfinished somehow. I stuck out my hand. "O.K.?"

He eyed my outstretched hand, but he would not take it. I stuck it back into my pocket.

"What's wrong?" I said. "How can I make it up to you?"

"It's not what happened at the drugstore. That was just the last straw."

"Then what is it?"

"It's what you're getting ready to do. Lilly Fentrice is a good kid. She's going to hate your guts when she finds out you're using her."

Somewhere in my chest a large black cavity opened up. "Aw, come off it, Bull! Don't be so self-righteous."

"Look," he said, "this started out with just you and me. We've done worse things, I guess, but we always knew ahead of time what the stakes were. We never did anything if we weren't willing to take the consequences."

"So?"

"What I'm saying is that we do what we do with our eyes open, but Lilly is blind as a bat—and the fact that she's stuck on you doesn't help matters."

"What do you mean, stuck on me?" I was shaken, but I couldn't let him know. "That's stupid. She doesn't trust me as far as she can throw a feather."

"Maybe. But she's still stuck on you, and if you play her for a fool, you're going to do a lot of damage. I don't want to be a part of that."

"Well, what do you want me to do about it—junk my whole plan? Just when everything is working in my favor? Dammit, Bull, we aren't going to kidnap Nisbett. It's just a little practical joke! Why do you have to be so serious all of a sudden?"

74

"I've got to go finish my supper."

"Go ahead! And just remember—nobody's making you hang around."

"O.K. I'll remember that."

The door slammed behind him. A peal of thunder answered, rumbling across the sky. I went down the steps and out into the street, my eyes watering in the blowing dust. Coming here had been a mistake. Bull was crazy. Couldn't he see how funny it was going to be? Lilly would think it was funny too, once it happened. The large black cavity in my chest yawned wider. I began to run. I ran all the way to Felker Street without stopping.

The rain began to fall in large spattering drops just as I reached our porch. I stood there a moment, breathing hard and trying to decide whether to go into the dining room to face the music immediately or to go upstairs and make myself presentable first. My stomach growled. I chose to face the music.

They were in the middle of a heated conversation when I came into the dining room. G.C.'s face was flushed. His right hand was balled into a fist beside his plate. Mother's mouth was tightly pursed, as though she had bitten down on something sour. Dad glared at G.C. My entrance stopped their voices, but their anger went on and on in their eyes, and I got it from all three of them.

Dad laid his knife and fork deliberately across his plate as a signal that the meal was at an end. Mother placed her napkin in the napkin ring. Only G.C. didn't seem to care one way or another that I had finally arrived.

"Did you forget," said Dad, "that this is Wednesday?"

Rats! Wednesday evening was prayer meeting. I

75

hadn't given it a thought. "Yessir. I forgot." My stomach growled loudly.

"Go upstairs, wash your face and hands, and be ready in ten minutes."

"But don't I . . . do I get any dinner?"

"I'm afraid it's too late for that. Perhaps missing dinner will help you make it a point to be prompt from now on."

I ducked my head and backed out of the dining room. I didn't want to hear a sermon before I had to.

Fifteen minutes later we were walking to the First Baptist Church in a torrent of rain, bundled up in umbrellas, raincoats, and overshoes. Mother and Dad walked in front. G.C. and I followed like a couple of baby ducks. G.C. looked as though he would like to kill someone. I wasn't in a particularly talkative mood myself. The rain coated my face and dripped down into my collar. I was tired, wet, hungry, and generally miserable. The day's events kept floating to the top of my mind to irritate me, like bugs in a glass of milk. The last thing I needed was to sit in church and hear a discourse by the Reverend Duncan.

In the vestibule we took off the dripping coats and overshoes. I watched absently as the maroon carpet darkened under the steady rivulet from the point of Mother's umbrella which she had hung upside down from a peg. The odor of damp clothes, hair, and carpet mingled in a single mustiness. I wrinkled my nose against it. Maybe it wouldn't have bothered me if my stomach hadn't been so empty.

Prayer meetings are not exactly what you'd call overcrowded, even on an evening when the weather is decent. This time only the sticklers were there, and people like G.C. and me who were there because coming was easier than rebellion. The Reverend

76

Duncan walked in from the side door and sat in the chair behind the pulpit. He rested his head in his hands and closed his eyes. I wondered was he praying or just showing off. He was a short rectangular person with balding head and rimless eyeglasses. I found him tiresome.

After Miss Quentin's rendition of "Sweet Hour of Prayer," he got up soberly and welcomed those of us who had "braved the elements." The Reverend Duncan always had a hard time speaking plainly. He intoned even the simplest sentences as though they were part of a sermon. That way you couldn't tell when his sermon actually began. One minute he'd be welcoming and making announcements and the next, he was deep into Sin.

"I wish to speak tonight on the subject of betrayal," he began. "We all know how our Lord was betrayed by a trusted friend. He was, in fact, betrayed by a number of his friends in the moment when he most needed their faith and loyalty."

I suppressed a sigh and pulled one of the hymnals out of the pew rack. There's a game we guys play with the hymns called Under the Covers. We read the title of the hymn and then add the words "under the covers." We come up with some nifty sentences. For instance, "How Tedious and Tasteless the Hours . . . under the covers." Or "When I Can Read My Title Clear . . . under the covers." It is a good game for building up pressure. Finally a real humdinger like "Love Lifted Me" explodes us into uncontrollable snorting and wheezing. We usually get a lecture from our parents after church, but it is worth it.

I opened the hymnal to page 102 and poked G.C. I was about to point to the title "Look, Ye Saints! The Sight Is Glorious" when Dad reached over Mother, took the hymnal away from me, and set it in the rack.

I folded my hands across my belly and leaned back against the hard pew. My shoulder blades ached. So did my empty stomach, and my head. I was enraged at the world's oppressiveness. Fun is a Sin.

"There is no pain," the Reverend Duncan was saying, "like the pain of one who has been betrayed. That was probably one of the greatest burdens our Saviour carried to the cross with him. In his hour of stress when he asked them to stay awake with him while he prayed, they didn't take him seriously. Instead, they went to sleep . . . "

I resisted the urge to make snoring noises and wondered dully why he had picked such a topic. It didn't have anything to do with anything.

Suddenly in a sustained pause between the Reverend Duncan's paragraphs, my stomach growled long and loud. Dad moved nervously in the pew. G.C. turned red. There was a general shifting of bodies, as though people feared my stomach's growls would call out answering responses from their own. My heart leaped at this new prospect. I began surreptitiously to mash against my stomach so that it would growl all the louder.

Then G.C. put out a hand and clamped his fingers hard just above my knee. I choked back a yell and punched him in the ribs. Needless to say, my parents did not take kindly to all this. When G.C. and I had finally ceased our soundless scuffling I became aware of Dad's heavy breathing, as though through flaring nostrils. No telling what was in store for me when we finally got home. I gave up with a sigh and sat limp through the remainder of the ordeal.

We trudged home in a misty drizzle, Mother and Dad walking in front as before. G.C., instead of giving me the hell I expected, was silent and morose. My steps slowed and so did his until the folks were far enough ahead to be out of earshot.

"What's the matter?" I asked.

"Nothing."

"It didn't look like Nothing when I walked in tonight. With your fist balled up like that I thought you were about to punch Dad in the nose."

G.C. didn't deny it.

"You must have told them something they didn't want to hear," I said.

"Look, dammit, it's none of your business!" His words lashed at me. Under the streetlight I could see his face, contorted with misery. It scared me. What reason did G.C. have to be miserable? He had what he wanted. He never had to endure Dad's scorn. People never said to him, with accusation in their tone, "You could do so much better if you *applied* yourself!"

We walked a bit farther in silence. My mind played over the scene at Bull's house.

"Dolores Clammett wanted to know if you were all right," I said, to make conversation.

G.C. halted in midstride and grabbed my arm. His fingers were like steel. "What did you say?" His voice sounded strange, like a rubber band pulled taut.

"I went to the Clammetts' to see Bull. That's why I was late to dinner. Dolores answered the door, and she asked me if you were all right. I thought from the way she asked it that you had been sick and had to go home from work or something." I pushed at his hand and he released his grip. "You don't have to make a federal case of it, do you?"

He didn't reply. We plunged on in the rain.

"Look," I tried again. "Did I do something?"

79

G.C. shook his head.

"Because if I did, I want to know. I'll undo it if I can. We used to be pretty good buddies once."

"It's not anything you did or didn't do." I could tell his face was turned in my direction even though I couldn't see it in the dark. I only heard the sadness in his words. "Just forget it, will you? I don't want to talk about it."

"Yeah. O.K." There was a lump just under my collar that wouldn't go up or down, even when I swallowed. I felt as though I were walking in the drizzling rain all by myself.

8

MOTHER WASN'T PREPARED for me to be ready for school Thursday morning before eight o'clock. She couldn't have been more distraught if the sun had come up in the west.

"What is it?" she asked worriedly when I came downstairs dressed for breakfast and she had had to call me only once. "What's the matter?"

"Nothing. Why should anything be the matter?" I threw up my hands. "Some people are never satisfied!"

She ignored my histrionics. "I hope you aren't planning to do anything rash on account of what happened last night." She was referring to the fact that Dad had ordered me to bed as soon as we got home without even so much as a cold biscuit for nourishment. Mother considers that to be cruel and unusual punishment. She has great investment in the staff of life and all that. She did not know that I had an emergency cache of candy bars in the toe of my outgrown bedroom shoes.

"You mustn't take your father's punishments too seriously," she went on, sitting down with me at the table while I ate my cereal. "I know he may seem too strict, but when you grow older you'll thank him."

I doubted that, but it wasn't worth arguing about. I suppose she has to believe it since he's her husband and she has to live with him. I assured her that I wasn't planning to run away from home. Actually, I had other things on my mind. I intended on that morning, to present a newly humbled, self-effacing Will Thomas to Miss Lauderbach.

It seemed strange to arrive at school almost before anyone else. The playground was quiet and deserted. The rain had settled the dust, and here and there patches of green struggled up between the rocks and gravel. I stood on the main walkway and looked up at the letters etched in the cement over the door.

RIVERTON HIGH SCHOOL

1916

I felt no surge of patriotism or satisfaction. I didn't have many pleasant memories of my experiences within those walls—nothing to hold me. Come May 1924, I was going to bid it good-by with much rejoicing.

The large clock in the hallway had just clicked eight fifteen when I stepped into Miss Lauderbach's room. She was at her desk as I knew she would be, working intently over piles of papers and murmuring unintelligibly as she did so. Her too-brown hair was pulled back and fastened in a bun at the back of her neck. Her face was thin and severe, but not mean. I wondered sometimes whether Miss Lauderbach slept at the school, or what it was that compelled her to stay so late each afternoon and enticed her to return before anyone else the next morning. During her long career she has taught just about every subject, except possibly chemistry and industrial arts. She has taught me elocution, Latin, and history. I have barely squeaked by each time, for one reason or another. However, I have been very careful not to offer excuses to Miss Lauderbach. She is nobody's fool. And besides, I have learned a lot in her classes, in spite of myself.

I stood inside the doorway and waited for her to notice that I was there.

After a moment she looked up from her work. If she was surprised to see me, she didn't show it.

"Good morning, William. What can I do for you?"

"I wondered—do you have a minute to spare?" I came forward. Humbly. Self-effacing.

"I believe so." She put her red pencil aside and looked at me curiously. "Sit there in the front seat."

I slid into the seat and folded my hands upon the desk top. I was careful to look at them and not at her.

"Miss Lauderbach, I'm not sure how to say what I'm about to say."

"William, I find it hard to believe that you haven't thought out every word—that you not only know what you will say, but what *I* shall say also."

That shook me. I looked at her then, and saw humor in her eyes. For a passing instant I wanted to back out.

"Well?" she said.

I took a deep breath and steeled myself to endure her sharp gaze. Some perverseness in me wanted her to see through me—to catch me at the outset.

"I'm giving up," I said, looking her straight in the eye. "Surrendering."

Miss Lauderbach blinked. "To whom, pray?"

"To you—to the school—to everybody, I guess."

83

"I don't understand."

"Miss Lauderbach, you know very well that I haven't done anything these past three years in high school except fool around. I haven't studied as I should. I've spent more time and energy trying to think of ways to get out of work than I have actually working. And I'm not going to do it anymore. I've been a disappointment to my family, to my teachers, to myself. I want to turn over a new leaf."

"Why?" she asked simply.

"I'm ashamed." I said it without a moment's hesitation. "I realize that a sudden about-face is always suspicious, especially when a person isn't very trustworthy. But a guy has to begin somewhere."

Miss Lauderbach's eyes were full of questions, but she did not ask them. "It's very admirable of you to want to make this change," she said. "You realize, of course, that it isn't going to affect your grades this year, what with the end of school so near."

"Yes, I know that. I was afraid you'd think that's why I came."

She frowned. "Why did you come to *me?*"

I leaned forward. "Because telling you is part of the bargain I've made with myself. Every time I'm around you, I'll remember that you know what I'm trying to do. It'll be harder to backslide."

"I see." She fiddled with a ruler on her desk. Her eyes were inscrutable.

I stood up. "Thank you for listening. I hope—that is, if you can think of ways that I can prove myself, I'll be glad to do whatever I can."

"Thank you, William. I'll keep that in mind."

I smiled at her, and then I reached over and put out my hand. The unflappable Miss Lauderbach took it awkwardly. Her handclasp was not as firm as I expected.

Probably the person most rattled by my early appearance at school that day was Miss Timothy. I was the first person to come into her classroom. I thought she was going to have a stroke.

"Here is my theme." I laid it on her desk. It was a masterpiece of neatness. I had sat up the night before after everyone else was asleep, munching chocolate bars and copying the essay in my best hand.

She looked at me, then at the papers.

"What are you up to, William Thomas?"

I took a step backward. "Up to? Miss Timothy, I don't know what you mean. I am here—on time. Nay, *early* for a change, with my homework assignment completed. Unless I am sadly mistaken, this is what you've been trying to get me to do for months. I'm not up to anything!"

"It will be a cold day in July before I shall believe that," she said with great weariness. "However, I suppose one shouldn't look a gift horse in the mouth."

She gathered up the essay and put it in her portfolio.

I was indignant. I wanted to ask how she ever expected a guy to change if she wouldn't believe the change when it happened. It was their fault—all of them, I fumed—for expecting me to behave the way I had always behaved. By George, they deserved what they got! I whirled and stalked to my desk, forgetting for a moment that I *was* up to something.

Maybe Miss Timothy can read minds.

"William, don't misunderstand me. Look at it from my point of view, if you can. I have been victimized by your behavior over the past months. Naturally, it has made me wary. Believe me, I welcome a real change."

She came down hard on the "real." I admit I was impressed by her straightforwardness.

The rest of the school day was so-so. I struck up a conversation with Paul Nisbett. I studiously avoided Bull, but it was not easy. Even when my back was turned I could feel his eyes upon me, judging. I wooed Lilly with exorbitant sweetness, apologizing for my behavior in the drugstore. She forgave me instantly. Even when John Norman and Billy Drew put smushed earthworms between the pages of Retta Kilburn's lab manual, I did not participate. I made a point of being hard at work on my side of the lab when it happened.

By 3:00 P.M. I was completely worn out. Being good taxed my strength. I wasn't at all sure, after this day, that I could keep up the show until Commencement.

I dropped my books at home and went to work by way of Hildebrande Avenue. As I approached the Benson mansion I wondered absently whether Mrs. Benson had yet seen fit to transfer a few of her excess dollars to Aunt Jessica's bank account. Perhaps I would never know, but it didn't matter just then. I was too tired.

Suddenly I was aware of voices arguing behind the roses that wound themselves around the trellis in the garden. The last thing I expected to see was Dr. Benson bursting from behind the roses and barreling down the walk toward the gate, thumping his gold-headed cane upon the flagstones. His jaw was set, his eyes grim slits behind his spectacles. His thin white hair was not covered by a hat. His brown suit was

86

disheveled. He resembled an old Teddy Roosevelt. When he reached the gate he looked about wildly and then focused upon me. The grimness became an ordinary frown.

"Yes?" His voice was a demanding roar. "You want something, young man?"

"No, sir." In desperation I looked down at the dirt and rocks under my feet.

"Have you lost something?"

"I—dropped a quarter." That was no lie. I did drop a quarter once. Just not right there, right then.

"A quarter?" Dr. Benson sounded interested, even sympathetic. "Did you find it?"

"Yes, sir."

He looked disappointed. I began to move away. "One minute, young man. What's your name?"

"Will Thomas, sir. Gregory Thomas' son."

"Oh, yes. Of course. Sorry. You've grown a bit. It's hard to keep up with you young fellows. You know how it is. I'm glad you found your quarter. It may not seem like much to you, but quarters make dollars."

By now he was fussing with the gate latch. His pale, bony hands shook slightly and I wondered whether I should offer to help unfasten the latch.

"Yes, indeed. Hold on to what you earn. Do you have a job?"

"Yes, sir. I work at Aunt Jessica's bookstore and at the public library."

He had succeeded in undoing the gate. He came outside where I was and pulled it shut behind him. "Do you mean Mrs. Brassey? She's your aunt?"

I nodded.

"Pity! Meddlesome woman!" He turned on his heel and walked away without another word, heading in the direction I also intended to go. I looked after his bareheaded, retreating figure, stumping along in the rumpled brown suit, his cane banging the ground at every step. Obviously it had been a mistake to mention Aunt Jessica's name in his presence.

As if that were not enough, Mrs. Benson came tumbling around the side of the house. Her skirts hampered her somewhat, but still she was making good time for a lady.

"William! William, thank goodness you're here! Have you seen Dr. Benson?"

"Yes, ma'am." I pointed. "He just left."

She flung open the gate and came out to stand beside me, shading her eyes as she looked down the street. Dr. Benson turned left at the corner and disappeared from view.

"Oh, dear!" It was almost a sob. She was panting and holding her side from the running. "Oh, *dear!*"

"Is there something I can do?" I shifted from one foot to the other and wished I had taken another route to work. "I'm going to work now. I could catch up with him, if you want—"

She seemed to realize then where she was and who I was and how she must look. By sheer willpower she straightened her face and made herself calm.

"No. No, I think not. Thank you just the same."

She appeared to be waiting for me to take my leave before she went back inside the gate. I turned to go, thinking how strange it was that a person could feel dismissed from a street, even in a free country.

9

ALTHOUGH I HURRIED, I did not see Dr. Benson when I got down to Main Street. For a gentleman his age he certainly seemed to have covered the ground fast. I finally concluded that he had gone to his office.

When Dr. Benson first moved back to Riverton he rented the office. I thought it strange, since he was in his seventies and had no intention of continuing his medical practice. But when I mentioned it to Dad, he chuckled and said maybe the doctor had rented the office to get away from his wife. I found that hard to believe. Mrs. Benson was not the sort of person a fellow would need to get away from. I mentioned it to Aunt Jessica. She snorted and said that Dr. Benson was just a foolish old man.

So now I dismissed the whole incident. Maybe Dr. Benson was indeed a foolish old man. At any rate, he had lived a long life and probably he was slipping.

Not until I had my hand on the door handle of the bookstore did I see the CLOSED sign hanging just in front of my eyes inside the glass. The shade was drawn, the door locked. I shook it and the sign rattled against the glass. I shaded my eyes and tried to peer inside through the display window, but the stacks of stationery boxes obstructed my view. The place appeared deserted. In all my years of working for her, Aunt Jessica had never closed the shop in the middle of the afternoon. She always had someone to come in if she had to be away.

After a minute I walked across the street to Marcus' Hardware.

G.C. and Dolores Clammett were unpacking crates of rifle cartridges, but they weren't being very businesslike about it. They were laughing a lot and teasing each other. Once they both grabbed the same box and pretended to fight over it. They didn't notice me at first, which is probably why they acted so embarrassed when G.C. finally looked up and saw me standing there.

"Is there something I can do for you?" He was sarcastic and brusque, but I knew it was because he was feeling silly, so I didn't make anything of it. Dolores' face was pink, and she excused herself and went to the back of the store where the office was.

"Yeah," I said. "Aunt Jessica's not at the store. There's a CLOSED sign on the door."

"Well, what do you want me to do about it—call the police?"

"No. I just thought maybe you'd know where she was."

"Well, I don't." He turned his back on me and shoved cartridge boxes rapidly upon the shelves. "Maybe she's sick."

"Who—Aunt Jessica?"

"There's always a first time for everybody."

"Are you *sure* you haven't seen her all day?"

"I'm *sure!*" His eyes flickered toward the back of the store, where Dolores had disappeared. "I got more important things on my mind."

"Yeah. I can see that." I turned and started out.

90

"I'm going to try to find her. At least keep an eye open, *if* you can spare the time from your pressing duties."

I ignored his answering growl and left. I worried all the way to Aunt Jessica's house, which was at the west end of Main Street. It sat back from the sidewalk like a sunken eye, all grimy with train smoke and covered with ivy. I realized, as soon as I twisted the bell handle, that it had been a long time—months, in fact—since I had been there. When I was a little guy I came to visit her often. She fed me cinnamon toast in her greasy kitchen that smelled of gas, and we had talked about important things—or at least they seemed important to me then. She never worried much about crumbs scattered or milk spilled. The fact was, she created so much debris herself that mine was not very noticeable.

She didn't come to the door. I waited a bit, then picked my way around to the back through overgrown brambles and grasses. I had the feeling sometimes that the foliage supported the house and that if it were cut back or trimmed the house would fall down.

The back door was locked too. No one answered my knock.

At that point what had been merely a nagging anxiety became a full-blown fear. I thought about Aunt Jessica lying on the floor in there, with a broken hip, unable to summon help. Or maybe a burglar had come and gone, leaving her unconscious or seriously injured. I began walking, fast, in the direction of Riverton Cotton Gin.

The Gin is the largest in the county. It has made a lot of money for Mr. Nisbett, but the business offices are unpretentious, if not downright grubby. Dad's office, like the others, is in a wooden building and is about the size of a matchbox. Lint from the ginning settles over everything. Some days Dad comes home with his good black coat several shades lighter than it should be. Mother spends a lot of time using the whisk broom.

Mrs. Preston, the company secretary, sat at her typewriter behind a long counter. When she saw me her eyebrows climbed two inches. I glanced down and saw that my shirttail was out and my socks were sagging down into my shoes. My pants were prickly with brambles and burrs from Aunt Jessica's overgrown yard. I shoved my shirttail into my pants and tried to smooth my hair down all at once.

Mrs. Preston rose and went to knock on Dad's office door. "Your son William is here, Mr. Thomas. Will you see him?" A moment passed while he got up from his desk and came to the door. He looked past her at me and frowned.

"William! Where in the world have you been? Come into my office at once."

I went in, feeling Mrs. Preston's eyes upon me all the way. My breathing had slowed some by that time. I opened my mouth to tell him why I was there, but he was already doing the talking for both of us.

"Now, what is the meaning of this, coming to my place of business looking like a ragamuffin? What would Mr. Nisbett think if he saw you? Suppose someone important had been here when you arrived?"

For me, the whole day suddenly ignited and blew up.

"The house is on fire!" I yelled.

He went pale. I already regretted my rashness, but it was too late to take the words back. I reached out and stopped him as he started toward the door.

"No, it's not on fire!" I said between my teeth, "but it could have been. Why couldn't you wait for me to tell you why I was here?"

Mrs. Preston stuck her head in the door. "Is everything all right?"

"Yes. Quite. Thank you, Mrs. Preston." Dad made shooing motions and she went back out. "Now, William. Have the goodness to explain—"

"Aunt Jessica's disappeared. When I went to work the shop was closed. I went to the house and knocked and called. Nobody was there either, or at least if—"

I didn't even want to think about the "if."

"Sit down," Dad said. I obeyed, flopping into the battered leather chair in front of his desk. He went around to his side and sat in the revolving chair that squeaked when he moved.

"Now—you say Jessica has disappeared. But what you really mean is that you don't know where she is. Is that correct?"

I nodded. It was hard to look at him. "Dad, you know she never closes the store in the middle of the afternoon, especially now, when she needs all the business she can get. Besides, if she had planned to be gone, she would have told me."

Dad sighed. "I appreciate your concern for your aunt, but I have known her for a very long time. More than likely she is at an all-day meeting of the WCTU or at a Confederate Memorial Day observance. I shouldn't worry about her if I were you. Jessica is quite capable of taking care of herself."

"But she would have told me—"

"Don't overestimate your importance, William. You're her employee, not her business partner. Why don't you run along home and tidy up a bit. You look terrible."

I felt suddenly dull and tired, like the time I had run my heart out in the seventh-grade relay race and our team lost anyway. I got up and went out.

"William—" he called.

I didn't bother to reply.

"Drop by again, William," Mrs. Preston said brightly. "We don't see enough of you around here!"

I don't even remember what I said.

When I got home Mother met me in the hallway full of questions about what I was doing there at that time of day.

"Aunt Jessica wasn't at work. The store was closed."

Mother's eyes widened. I could see that she appreciated the unusual nature of the situation. "For heaven's sake!" she murmured. "Didn't she leave a note?"

I shook my head. "She wasn't at home, either. I went over there and knocked and called, but she never answered."

"I see." Mother's hands fluttered to her apron and found comfort in twisting its loose folds. "Well, when your father comes home perhaps he—"

"I went to the Gin and told him. He didn't seem to be too worried about her—said she could take care of herself."

Mother's face showed a mixture of concerns. I could see she was struggling with her natural inclination to be fearful about Aunt Jessica's unexplained vanishing and her equally natural instinct to defer to Dad's judgment in all things. The latter finally won over. Her face cleared.

"Well, if he's not worried, then I'm sure every-

94

thing is all right," she said, smoothing the apron as a kind of signal to me that I shouldn't bother myself about it. "You run along upstairs and do your school-work. I'll call you when dinner's ready. It's fried chicken tonight." She beamed at me, knowing fried chicken was my favorite. I figured she was trying to make up for no dinner at all the night before.

I went to my room, but instead of sitting down at the desk I lay across the bed and closed my eyes. The day swirled through my head—the session with Miss Lauderbach seemed a hundred years ago. I slept and had confused dreams of Dr. and Mrs. Benson chasing each other around their manicured gardens while Dad sat in a brown suit by the iron gate saying over and over, "Don't worry. Don't worry."

I woke up when the door to my room opened softly and G.C. whispered, "Will? You awake?"

"Sure. Come in. What time is it?" I sat up and wiped the sleep from my eyes.

"Not quite six. Dad's not home yet." He came in, shutting the door behind him, and sat on the edge of the bed.

"Dad's not home? Good gosh—first Aunt Jessica and now Dad. What's going on?"

"You never found her then?" G.C. sighed. His chin sank to his chest. "I wasn't much help to you this afternoon. I'm sorry. I know what the old lady means to you. I could've been more sympathetic."

I flung myself off the bed and went over to the window, turning my back on him. "She's not all that much to me. I just work for her. She's Dad's sister, not mine. I'm just looking out for my job—"

My own words stung my mouth. I could not go on.

"Well," he said after a moment, "I guess I was mistaken. I thought it was Aunt Jessica you cared about." The bedspring squeaked as he got up. Seconds later the door slammed. I listened to his footsteps going along the hall to his room. And then I leaned my head against the window frame and bawled like a little kid.

Dad finally arrived at six thirty, but he was usually so punctual—and so demanding of punctuality in others—that he might as well have come in at midnight. My eyes felt puffy, but by that time they didn't look too bad in the mirror. I kept my head down as much as possible, pretty sure no one would notice.

"I'm sorry, Edith," Dad said, taking off his hat and handing it to Mother. I couldn't tell whether he was agitated because he was late or because we were there to witness his lateness. "I stopped by Jessica's on the way home from the office. She wasn't there."

An ominous silence filled up the dining room. Dad did not look at all calm. A small wisp of hair stood out just above his ear. He went to his place at table and sat. The vertical crease between his eyebrows had deepened. G.C. and I exchanged glances—Dad had not washed his hands. Mother was aware of it, too, but none of us dared say a word.

We bowed our heads for the Blessing.

"Oh, Lord, our God," Dad began. His voice was dry and thin. "We thank Thee for all Thy many blessings. Help us to use them in Thy service. Amen."

I brought my head up slowly, not sure whether to trust my ears. Mother and G.C., from the expressions on their faces, were equally amazed at the brevity of the prayer. Dad tried to look as though nothing were different.

"Well," he said, "can we eat, or must we wait until the food gets cold?"

Flustered, Mother served the plates. For a long

time the silence continued unbroken except for the noises of chewing and swallowing and the clink of silverware upon china plates.

"What do you suppose has happened?" Mother asked in a few minutes. "Do you think we should call the police?"

"Call the police! Edith, that's ridiculous. Jessica isn't in any sort of trouble—I'm sure of it. We're just accustomed to her following the same routine day after day. It only goes to show what creatures of habit we are."

"What are you going to do if she shows up dead in a ditch somewhere?" G.C. asked calmly.

For the second time that day I saw Dad turn deathly pale. He laid his fork upon his plate and sat staring at the food. "G.C., that was uncalled for. You shouldn't worry your mother with such comments."

Mother was taking it very well, actually. I didn't doubt that G.C. had asked the question that was on her mind.

"Dad," I said, "could we call Mrs. Benson? Maybe she's heard something from Aunt Jessica."

"It won't be necessary. We don't want to trouble the Bensons."

"But Aunt Jessica is her best friend."

"I'm sure that Mrs. Benson is very cordial to Jessica," Dad said, "but 'best friends' is overstating it, don't you think?"

"No, sir. They're as close as Bull and me—"

"Bull and I," Dad corrected. Mother's mouth tightened.

"No, that's not right either," I mumbled. Suddenly I wasn't hungry anymore. "May I be excused please? I don't feel like eating."

"Your eyes *do* look puffy," Mother said. She

reached to lay a hand on my forehead, but I pulled away.

"I don't have a fever—just no appetite."

"Your mother went to a great deal of trouble to prepare this meal. The least you can do is eat it." Dad picked up his fork again. I was reminded of the times when he had persuaded me to take a dose of quinine or castor oil by taking one himself.

"Maybe he's too upset to eat." Even though G.C.'s words were quiet, I had the strange feeling that he was shouting at Dad. "Telephone Mrs. Benson."

Dad seemed to swell. "G.C., Mrs. Benson and your aunt are not social equals. I hope you realize that. It would be a great intrusion on my part to call."

G.C. stood up suddenly and flung his napkin upon the table. "I can't stand it!" He choked on the last word. His sad, angry eyes seemed to fill up the room, the house. He lifted his arms and dropped them again hopelessly.

"Social equals!" he said in a strangled voice. "If you had your way, we could only love and be loved by a boxful of people who were exactly like us. How will we ever grow? How will we ever be different?"

I was stunned by his eloquence. It seemed to me that he was speaking of something much larger than Aunt Jessica's friendship with Mrs. Benson.

"G.C., don't talk that way to your father!" Mother sounded frightened. "Why don't you just eat your dinner and . . ."

"I'm moving out, first thing tomorrow. I should've done it long before now."

"That isn't necessary or advisable," Dad said.

"It's both of those," G.C. shot back.

"What does all this have to do with Jessica?" Mother asked wonderingly. She sounded so sincere

98

and serious in the middle of all the tension and furor that I couldn't help laughing outright. Unfortunately, Dad took it wrong.

"William, if you can't control yourself, you may as well leave the table!"

So I did. I got up and went out, and G.C. was right behind me. I was laughing, but my eyes were wet, and seeing G.C.'s grim sadness didn't help any.

"How well do you know Mrs. Benson?" he asked as we went upstairs.

"Pretty well. She comes to the library a lot. She's no snob."

"Then if I were you, I'd telephone her. Right now."

I followed him to his room. "How can I do that without Mother and Dad knowing?"

"Let them see you do it."

"That's easy for you to say! *I'm* not moving out. Dad would take away every privilege I have—and a few I don't have."

G.C. shrugged and turned his back on me. He opened a drawer and began tossing clothes out upon his bed. "Suit yourself," he said.

I hung around a minute or two, but when I realized he was ignoring me I went to my own room. I sat on the edge of the bed and thought about going down-stairs and making that phone call. I imagined Dad's eyes on me as I told the operator the number—his fury, his embarrassment. I couldn't take it, even in my imagination. After a while I heard Mother come upstairs and knock on G.C.'s door.

At first their voices were only a murmur and I couldn't understand them. Then Mother said, "Please, G.C. He's so terribly worried. He's not him-self. Don't do anything you'll regret—"

99

"Why can't he say he's worried, then? Why can't he be a plain human being sometimes instead of pretending he's God Almighty who can make all things turn out right?"

"G.C., don't talk like that!"

"G.C., don't talk like that!" he mimicked.

I wished that he wouldn't be so hard on Mother. She couldn't help how she was. Dad had trained her to jump.

"I have to go downstairs now," she said. "Can't I tell your father you've changed your mind?"

"Hell, no!" he said roughly. I could imagine her wincing at that. "I'm packing tonight. Tomorrow I'll get some friends to come move the stuff away."

"But where will you go?"

"Don't worry about it. I'll get a place."

I thought about G.C.'s room standing empty. I lay down on the bed again and buried my face in the pillow. A long time afterward I fell asleep.

10

IT WAS THE MIDDLE OF THE NIGHT, or so it seemed, and there were voices in the hall outside my door. At first I was confused, thinking that Mother and G.C. must be continuing their conversation, but then I realized one of the voices was Aunt Jessica's. I sat straight up in bed, staring into the dark, trying to figure whether I was awake or dreaming.

"Jessica, he's worn out," my mother was pleading. "Please can't it wait until tomorrow morning?"

"No. Absolutely not. He has done a terrible thing. I want to see him now!"

Then Dad spoke. "Jessica, this is ridiculous. The boy needs his sleep, and there's nothing he can do to change what has happened."

"That may be, but he needs to know the consequences of his irresponsible actions."

My mouth was drier than a stream bed in August. What were they talking about? What had I done?

The door opened and a sliver of light from the hall split the darkness. Mother slipped into the room and closed the door behind her.

"William, are you awake?"

"Yes, ma'am. What time is it? Where's Aunt Jessica been?"

"It's ten thirty, and I think you'd better get up and come downstairs. I'm sorry. I didn't want to wake you, but Jessica wants to see you."

"But what's it all about?"

"I don't really know, William. Just come down as soon as you can."

She went out and shortly I heard all their footsteps clumping raggedly down the stairs. I got up and pulled on the trousers I had flung over the chair. My hands shook so, my fingers could only fumble with the buttons.

Out in the light of the hall I wiped at my fuzzy eyes and went downstairs as slowly as I could, in no hurry to face whatever I was about to face. Vibrations of disapproval came at me from all sides. Mother had retreated to the piano stool behind the divan. Dad stood with his hands clasped behind him like a political orator about to launch on the world's longest speech. Aunt Jessica, looking tired and deflated, sat in the morris chair, her pocketbook upon her lap, her hat unintentionally tilted.

"Have a seat in that chair, William," Dad ordered. "We—Jessica has a few things to say to you."

I sat down slowly in the chair opposite her. "Where've you been?" I asked.

"*I* shall ask the questions," she said. "Listen to what I am about to tell."

"Yes, ma'am."

"This afternoon, about the time you usually come to work, the door to the shop burst open and in walked Edgar Benson. He was angry to the point of dementia."

She paused and looked closely at me, to be sure I was absorbing every word.

"Fortunately, no customers were there at the moment. He said slanderous things. I believe he was mad enough to throttle me, but rather than run out into the street for help and create a scene, I told him to calm down and we would talk like two rational adults, or he could leave!"

She spit out the words, moving her plump shoulders like a hen whose feathers have been doused with water.

"He agreed, if only to prove himself rational. I locked the door and put up the CLOSED sign so that our conversation wouldn't be interrupted."

So Dr. Benson had gone straight to the bookstore after I saw him at his gate. That was why I hadn't caught sight of him on Main Street.

"The first thing he said was that I was a trickster —a Smooth Operator, I believe were his exact words." She dabbed savagely at her eyes. I looked down at my bare toes and wished I was in bed asleep. Maybe I *was* asleep, dreaming. I wiggled one toe.

"He went on to say that I had been scheming for years to get my hands on his money in order to build a new library for this town. He said that I was pretending to be his wife's friend, hoping that if he died and left all of his money to her, I could influence her to endow the library. He went on to say that he had known these things for a long time, but had had no solid proof until this very day, when his wife had come to him and asked him, outright, for money for *me.*"

She stabbed at her bosom with her index finger. "Can you imagine such a thing?"

I shook my head dumbly, which was what I was expected to do.

"He said to me: 'You should be ashamed of yourself, putting Kate up to such tricks! You know that she

103

is a weak women, easily influenced by someone like yourself. Your library will not get a penny of my money, and furthermore I have told her that *she* will not get any either if she continues to consort with you!'"

Aunt Jessica turned to Dad. "I tell you, Gregory, if I were not well brought up, and a lady, I should have slapped his hairy old face!"

"What *did* you do?" I asked.

"I said to him, 'Edgar Benson, I have never mentioned to your wife anything about using your money for a public library—*never!* But in your present state of mind, I don't expect you to believe it. That is neither here nor there. You must know that I have never asked Kate for money. I would take an oath before all the archbishops of the world to that effect. I don't *need* money.'

"And then . . . *then,* William, is when he said: 'Aha! I knew I would catch you in your lie. You *do* need money, or you will lose your bookstore. I know that, because Kate *told* me!'"

She leaned forward and her blue eyes were stern and cold. "Now, William—would you be so kind as to tell me how Kate knew about my business affairs, since I did not tell her?"

I raised my eyes from my wiggling toes. My mind was as blank as it has ever been in all my life. I grabbed for this excuse and then that one, but none of them would do. What could I say?

"William, your aunt has asked you a question. Have the respect to answer!"

"Yes, sir." I licked my dry lips. Aunt Jessica's eyes held me as firmly as Judgment Day. I told them about Tuesday afternoon, and Mrs. Benson's invitation for lemonade and cookies.

104

"William Thomas, I am astounded at you!" Dad was practically apoplectic. "Didn't you realize Mrs. Benson was merely being polite—that she had no idea you would actually accept the invitation?"

I opened my mouth to reply but Aunt Jessica intervened. "You are mistaken, Gregory. Kate Benson is not from these parts. She doesn't issue invitations she doesn't mean." She turned back to me. "Now—continue. You went in with Kate."

"Yes. And she was really nice to me—treated me like a regular person."

"So you took advantage of her hospitality to further your cause."

"No, ma'am. We were just talking about one thing and another. She told me she was a school teacher. Then she remembered I was supposed to be working and apologized for keeping me—you know, like I was doing her a favor by coming in for a visit—"

Dad snorted. Aunt Jessica held up her hand for him to keep still.

"And then is when I told her. . . . I told her—" I looked up at the ceiling for inspiration.

"You told her what?"

"That it was O.K. because . . . I was probably working for nothing when I worked."

"William!"

My gaze slid down from ceiling to far wall. "And it seemed like the right time to tell her that you were having financial difficulties. I didn't ask her for money—honest I didn't. I only reported. And . . . and she was very concerned, as I thought she would be. She wanted to know why you hadn't told her, and I said I thought—"

"You thought?"

"—that you had too much pride." I forced myself

105

to look her in the eye when I said the words. It took more courage than you could believe.

Aunt Jessica's bosom heaved. "It is unfortunate, young man, that *you* don't have any pride at all. You cannot imagine the pain and problems you have caused!"

I bowed my head, not because I felt particularly contrite, but because that kept me from seeing the accusing eyes of Dad and Aunt Jessica. I thought perhaps she was overstating the case.

"Jessica, what did you do when Dr. Benson made his . . . ah . . . accusation?" Dad asked.

"I was stunned—which put me at a disadvantage. I said to him, 'My business affairs are my own concern. I do not inflict them upon anyone else, especially my dear friends. I have not told Kate anything of my business. I do not intend to. You can believe that or not. It's true.'

"He stood up then, and said of course he didn't believe it. That he expected me to lie. That anyone who had gone to such extremes to obtain money would not hesitate a moment about lying."

I had never felt so sorry for Aunt Jessica. She, who was honest to the point of being dangerous, and uncompromising to the point of submitting to torture rather than yield her ideals and principles, had been called a liar. She was overwhelmed by the fact that Dr. Benson believed she was one, and that she could not disprove it.

"He stormed out as he had stormed in, saying he was on his way to his office and from there to the bank—that he intended to alter his will so that there would be no way for any of his money to be used for a library. I cannot tell you how upset I was. I felt that I simply could not face anyone after his tirade. So I

106

left the sign on the door and sat at my desk and prayed until I felt calm enough to proceed. Then I went to the telephone and called Kate.

"As soon as she spoke I knew something terrible had happened. She began to weep. She kept saying over and over, 'I'm so sorry, Jess—so sorry!' I realized then I could do nothing over the telephone, so I told her I was on my way to her house and to instruct her arrogant butler to admit me as soon as I arrived.

"To make a long story short, I took a taxi to Kate's, not really sure what I was going to do, particularly if Edgar came while I was there. I should probably have hit him over the head with my umbrella. At any rate, she was waiting for me on the porch. She was in a terrible state. We went out to the garden to talk, and she told me that she had, indeed, asked for money on my behalf. You cannot imagine, Gregory, what courage that took."

Dad looked puzzled. "Courage? Why so?"

"Edgar Benson has never let the woman have a penny of her own. She has to ask for every cent, and must justify any expenditure, including household items."

"That sounds like good management to me," Dad said.

It was Aunt Jessica's turn to snort. "The poor woman can't even buy a bar of soap without asking for the few cents to pay for it! He won't even let her have a checking account of her own, and this is a man who has hundreds of thousands of dollars."

"Jessica, you exaggerate—about the business of not giving Mrs. Benson spending money, I mean. *You* know how scatterbrained women are about money. Probably in the past she has been extravagant—"

Aunt Jessica slapped her hand upon the leather

107

purse in her lap. "Gregory, you know nothing about it! I shall tell you the worst, although I expect it not to be repeated outside of this room."

Dad rolled his eyes toward the ceiling the same as I had done. "What is it, Jessica?"

"Edgar Benson is slipping. He imagines that his money is being squandered by all sorts of people. He suspects the bankers, his stockbrokers, the servants, and Kate in turn. He goes to the bank almost every day and asks to see his papers. He requires that they show him their records of his savings account balance and his checking account balance, to see if they agree with his own. He fears that he and Kate are on the verge of poverty. At one point a couple of months ago he refused to pay the servants, saying that they had already stolen from him more than they had earned. Kate was distraught, because the servants have been very good to her and very patient with him."

"Why didn't they quit?" I asked. "It's a free country. Nobody has to work for nothing anymore."

"Kate never let them know. They got their pay."

"You see?" said Dad. "Dr. Benson may be a bit eccentric, but he came through in the end, didn't he?"

"No," said Aunt Jessica. "Kate did."

"I thought she didn't have any money?"

"She didn't. She tried to borrow some, but of course she had no personal credit. He would have to cosign any loan agreement, so she abandoned that idea."

"Then how—?"

Aunt Jessica seemed uncomfortable. This time *she* looked up at the ceiling. I thought how beneficial it would be for all of us if certain aphorisms and maxims

108

—not to mention Scriptures—were written upon the rafters.

"She got the money from—a friend."

"See there," I said. "If Mrs. Benson can accept money from a friend, why can't you?"

Aunt Jessica regarded me as though I were slightly demented. "Who, pray, do you think the friend was who gave her the money?"

I opened my mouth, but before the words would come truth dawned—or should I say struck? I saw that Dad had been similarly affected. Mother was less amazed than we. I thought she showed more admiration than shock. We all remained silent while blocks and bolts fell into place. The reason Aunt Jessica was in financial difficulty was that she had loaned Mrs. Benson enough money to pay the servants, and Mrs. Benson was unable to pay it back.

"You can see," Aunt Jessica said quietly, "why Kate was so concerned that I might be in financial trouble. She felt responsible. In her desperation she did the most foolish thing ever, which was to ask Edgar outright for the amount of money she owed me, and when he demanded to know why she was asking for such a large sum, she told him the whole story, thinking that the embarrassment of being indebted to me, if nothing else, would cause him to give over the money. But she does not live with a rational man. He called her far worse things than he called me and said that she and I could get out of the mess as best we could. He told her he was going to put an end to my meddling once and for all. That's when he came to see me. I think it interesting that he never let on that he knew I had paid his servants' wages one month. So—that's the story. I stayed with her until after eight, when she was finally calmer. Edgar had not returned when I left there. She was about to send Richard out to look for him."

Dad's head moved back and forth as he tried to comprehend what he was hearing. His manner had changed. He no longer disbelieved Aunt Jessica.

"You could sue for the amount owed you," he said.

"Sue whom? Kate? She has no money. I will never cause her that anguish."

"But you have to look out for yourself!"

"I am managing. I am not without other resources, you know."

"Jessica, you did a very noble thing in helping Mrs. Benson, and I know you well enough to know that you did it selflessly, without any thought other than coming to the aid of a friend. But you see where it has gotten you—us. I imagine that if you had known then what you know now, you would have had second thoughts."

"No, indeed!" Aunt Jessica lifted her chin. "I should do it again in an instant!"

We all sat around some more, reflecting on what had been and what was to come.

"Well," said Dad at last, and his words were a sign, "I suppose there's no help for it, Jessica. We'll get the money somehow. I'll take out a loan tomorrow. I only hope that this will be a lesson to you—"

"Gregory, I don't want you to take out a loan. To-morrow morning I'm taking the train to Hadley. Alva has an old friend there who would, I believe, be of assistance. I want you to promise me you will do nothing and *say* nothing until I return."

It was hard for him, but Dad finally promised. Mother was greatly relieved. She got up from the piano and took several deep breaths.

110

"Who will mind the store in the morning, while you're away?" she asked.

Aunt Jessica did not hesitate. "I thought, Edith, that you could do that."

"Oh, Jessica, no! I couldn't." Mother fairly trembled.

"That's right," Dad said. "She couldn't. She's never worked in a store."

Aunt Jessica's pink face became pinker. "Gregory, that's unfair! Say you won't allow her, but pray don't say she *can't*. Edith's an intelligent, capable, and I might add *patient* woman. She can do anything you can do."

The statement struck Dad as absurd and he laughed. But just as quickly hushed when he saw the hurt on Mother's face.

"Why don't you do it, Mother?" I said. "It isn't hard, and I'll be along after school."

Mother's eyes darted from Aunt Jessica to Dad to me, and back to Aunt Jessica. Her nervous hands played with the folds of her skirt. "Well, I don't really know—but I'd like for all of this trouble to be straightened out as soon as possible. So . . . if my keeping the store is any help at all, I—I'll do it."

"Wonderful! I'll be by for you in the morning at eight thirty," said Aunt Jessica. "After I've shown you around the store, I'll take the ten thirty train to Hadley. I should be back before dark."

Suddenly Mother's face fell. "Oh, dear. I forgot. G.C. is moving out tomorrow. I really should be here to help him."

"Nonsense," said Aunt Jessica. "You told me it was his idea. Let him take care of it. He's not leaving town, is he?"

111

"No. That is, I don't think so."

"Then don't worry. A grown young man has no business living at home anyhow. It will be good for him to go elsewhere. It will teach him independence, and it will make him realize how good you two have been to him all these years."

Somehow when Aunt Jessica says things they make a lot more sense than before. Mother did not look absolutely convinced, but neither did she back out of her promise to mind the store.

When Aunt Jessica had departed at last, the three of us stood for a moment by the door looking at each other and trying to absorb the enormity of what we knew that nobody else in Riverton seemed to know. It was burdensome knowledge.

Dad said, "William, if you expended half the energy on your studies that you expend tending to business that is none of your concern, we should *all* be in better shape right now."

"Probably," I allowed. "I think I am going to reform. I'm very tired."

To my surprise he laughed and put a hand on my shoulder. "Go up to bed now. I'll see you in the morning."

I went, glassy-eyed with weariness. He called to me before I had reached the top of the stairs. "And don't look so worried. Things will get better."

"Oh, I don't doubt that," I said ruefully, "but only because they can't get worse."

11

BUT I WAS WRONG. I had dreamed that I was running as hard as I could to get to school before eight forty-five, but while I was still blocks away the bell began to ring. Try as I might, I could not seem to get to the school grounds. The street stretched longer and longer. I passed the same houses again and again, and the bell rang without stopping.

I woke up tense and tired, with the bell still ringing. Only it was the telephone and not the school bell. Just as I opened my eyes, it stopped.

I lay there for a couple of minutes, pressed down by a gray feeling. Gradually all the details of the night before came back, starting at the bottom of my mind and rising to the top like oil. Remembering made me want to turn over and bury my face in the pillow again.

Through the open window I heard the town clock strike six—pretty early for anyone to be telephoning. I wondered who it could be.

I rolled out of bed, padded barefoot down the hall to the bathroom, and splashed cold water in my face. Squinting in the mirror, I saw a fuzzy-faced guy with puffy eyes who seemed about as alert as a garden snail on a winter day. More cold water. I rinsed my

113

mouth with some of it, leaning elbows on the chilly porcelain. Even to stand upright was an effort.

Someone knocked on the bathroom door. I turned off the water tap. "Yeah? Who is it?"

"It's me," said G.C., his voice coming muffled through the closed door. "What's the matter, you sick or something?"

"No. I'm just washing my face."

"What're you doing up so early?"

"I couldn't sleep. What's it to you?"

"Nothing. I just want to shave when you get through your beauty treatment."

I started to make some smart remark, or at least to dawdle longer than I needed just to get back at him. But then I remembered he was leaving today for good. "I'm coming out right now." I opened the door.

He looked a bit the worse for wear—in fact, he had on the clothes he'd been wearing the night before. I guessed that he had slept in them.

"You going to work like that?"

"Maybe. What do you care?"

"I was just kidding. I don't care what you do," I said, and I meant it the right way, but he took it the wrong way. He slammed the door. In a moment I heard water running hard into the tub.

I dressed, combed my hair, and went downstairs. Dad was in his shirt sleeves pacing up and down in the hall. He looked very tired and bothered. He glanced up, startled.

"My word, William! What are you doing up at this hour?"

"The telephone woke me. I couldn't go back to sleep. What's up?"

Dad shook his head. "Unbelievable things. You'd

better go tell your mother you're up so she can serve your breakfast."

Mother came into the dining room from the kitchen with two steaming dishes. When she saw me she almost let go of them.

"The telephone woke me," I explained before she could ask the question. "I'll eat with you and Dad and G.C. if it's O.K."

"Of course!" She set the dishes on the table. "Did your father say who was on the telephone?"

"No, but he doesn't look too happy."

A little frown wrinkled Mother's brow. "I can't imagine. Do you suppose Jessica—?" But she didn't finish. Instead she went back to the kitchen.

I sat down at my place, feeling too sluggish and tired to speculate. In a few minutes Dad and G.C. came in together. Dad was telling him that Aunt Jessica was all right. G.C. smelled of bay-rum aftershave. There was a cheerful resoluteness about him that I had not seen in a long time. It made me envious, and a little sad. Why did he have to act so glad about moving out?

After the blessing, Mother heaped our plates with sausage and grits, scrambled eggs, biscuits, and homemade applesauce. Perhaps she hoped her food alone could make G.C. change his mind about leaving, but I knew he wasn't thinking about food.

Dad cleared his throat and then looked at each of us in turn. "I'm sorry to bring this up at breakfast, but I have some very serious news. Dr. Benson was found dead on his office steps early this morning by Constable Harris."

Mother gasped and pressed her hand over her mouth. G.C. whistled. I just sat there trying to take it in, seeing again Dr. Benson's disheveled figure

115

disappearing from view at the corner of Main and Hildebrande.

"Gosh, Dad—that's hard to believe! Are you sure?"

"Why should Mr. Nisbett call at six in the morning to tell me a monstrous lie?" Dad sounded wistful, as though he wished someone had indeed made a mistake.

"Mr. Nisbett? Why did *he* call?"

"He is a cousin of the doctor," Dad said. "Nearest next of kin."

"But why did he call *you?*" G.C. wanted to know. "Dr. Benson dying has nothing to do with us. We're not in the same social class, you know."

Dad, instead of taking offense at G.C.'s mocking tone, only looked worried. "I told you a while ago that Jessica was all right," he said to G.C., "but perhaps I should tell you everything." He related the events of the day before.

When he was done, G.C. said, "So the good doctor and Aunt Jessica had words, and he left her store in a stew. But does Mr. Nisbett know that? Is that why he called, because he thinks maybe Aunt Jessica did Dr. Benson in?"

"Good heavens, no! So far as I know, only the four of us and Jessica—and Mrs. Benson—know about the doctor's actions yesterday afternoon. It would seem to me to be most prudent for none of us to talk about it!"

"Then why?" G.C. persisted. "What does Mr. Nisbett want from you?"

Dad took a deep breath. "Before I answer that, I want to impress upon all of you the gravity of this situation. I'm not going to withhold any detail, because without this knowledge one of you might unwittingly throw our whole family into a complicated

116

and painful predicament."

He looked directly at me as he spoke. It was all I could do not to put my fingers in my ears. I didn't want to know. I didn't want to be responsible.

"Mr. Nisbett says the cause of the doctor's death is not certain. It appears that he had a heart seizure, but Mr. Nisbett wants an autopsy."

"Foul play suspected?" murmured G.C.

"Perhaps. The doctor was clutching a large leather satchel when he was found. The satchel was empty. Of course, it could have been empty all along, but there's no way of knowing for sure."

"Mr. Nisbett's not asking you to perform the autopsy, is he?"

"Don't be silly. The problem is that Mrs. Benson will not agree to an autopsy. He knows that Jessica is her good friend. He wants me to use my influence with Jessica in hopes that she will in turn persuade Mrs. Benson—"

"I hope you told him no," I said.

"No, I didn't. He's my employer."

"But Aunt Jessica's your sister!"

"I shall explain it to her as best I can," he said wearily. "She can do as she likes. I shall not try to influence her decision."

We sort of poked at our food for the remainder of breakfast. How had we gotten mixed up in this mess, anyhow? We knew too much, and somehow knowing too much can make you feel guilty, whether you are or not. After a while Dad excused himself to go call Aunt Jessica.

G.C. got up and said he still had some packing to do. I helped Mother clear the dishes off the table— and listened to her despairing clucks as she considered the Bensons. Afterward I went back to my room

117

and made up the bed. I hadn't been ready for school so far ahead of time since the day I entered first grade.

I could hear G.C. bumping about in his room. Tomorrow morning it would be quiet in there. I went and knocked on his door.

"It's me—Will. Can I come in?"

He opened the door and stood aside. Looking past him, I saw that he had stripped sheets from the bed and piled them in a corner. Two large suitcases and a couple of boxes stood in the middle of the room. The closet door was open. Nothing hung on the pole but a few scraggly coat hangers and an old overcoat of Dad's. The finality of it made me forget what I was going to say.

"Well?" he said.

I flopped my hands in a gesture of giving up. "When are you leaving?"

"Right now. I'm sending for the stuff later." He jerked up his arm and looked at his new wristwatch. "Damn! Already late!"

Before I could think of anything else to say, he had swished past me in a rush of air. I listened to his footsteps clattering upon the stairs and the front door slamming behind him.

Good-by, G.C.

I got my school books and went down to tell Mother and Dad I was leaving for school. Dad came out into the hallway just as I got to the foot of the stairs.

"I've just spoken with Jessica," he told me. "She was very upset. She won't go to Hadley today, but I was to tell you not to be late to work this afternoon anyway."

"All right," I said. "Did you—what is she going to do about . . . you know?"

"I didn't press her, William. And, William—"

"Yes, sir?"

"Please, today at school, be discreet."

Dad had never pleaded with me before about anything. Until now it had been a matter of his telling me what to do, but now instead of telling he was asking.

"All right. I'll keep quiet. Don't worry."

He seemed immensely relieved when he left.

School was awful that day. Dr. Benson's mysterious death was all anyone could think about. Rumors flew from person to person, from group to group. The number of versions of the tale multiplied by the hour. In an effort to keep quiet about it all, I stayed away from everyone, Lilly included. A dozen times I wanted to shout, "That's not true! It's nothing but gossip!" But that would only lead people to wonder what I knew that I wasn't telling. So I kept quiet. I noticed that Paul had not come to school and wondered if it was because he mourned the death of his kinsman or because his father had made him stay home.

I missed Bull. He, of all people, would eventually unearth the facts, going about on his grocery bike looking blank and listening hard. I thought wistfully of all the times the two of us had planned things together. What made this particular situation so hard for me was not having anyone to talk it over with.

But Bull never looked at me in the classroom, and he passed in the halls looking the other way. I told myself I didn't care—I could do without him. But I didn't feel any too good about seeing him talking with Lilly during lunch period. What were they talking about? My ears burned. I felt a desperate urgency about getting on with my plans to get in on Commencement. Time was passing. I now had two weeks to develop my perfect joke, and I needed Lilly to make it work.

During biology, the last period of the day, I found myself thinking about Lilly more than I needed to. I was supposed to be drawing the creature I viewed in the microscope, but my mind wandered.

It seemed to me that Lilly was a much *clearer* person than she had been. She had nice skin—not a lot of pimples like most of the girls in our class. Instead of being pale and invisible as in former times, now her cheeks were perpetually flushed and her eyes bright. Maybe it had something to do with Bull Clammett. Me and my bright ideas. I rested my forehead on the microscope's eyepiece and closed my eyes.

The next thing I knew my shoulder was being shaken roughly.

"Will, you're supposed to be working, not sleeping!"

Mr. Clark's white lab coat had a spot just above the second buttonhole. It was an old spot—iron rust, probably.

"I'm sorry," I said. "I don't know what came over me."

"Sleep, no doubt!" Mr. Clark said acidly. I bent my neck and looked up at his thin, smooth face. His hair, parted in the middle, lay plastered to his skull. I could tell by his look that he expected an argument and was braced.

"I apologize." I spoke in a low, polite voice. "I'll stay after school if I don't finish before the bell rings."

A tiny frown wrinkled the smooth forehead. Mr. Clark's eyes narrowed. He moved down the aisle, mumbling something about young people needing to go to bed at a reasonable hour. I blinked a few times to clear the fuzziness from my eyes and finished my drawing in record time. I couldn't see anything through the eyepiece, but from reading the text I knew what I was supposed to see, so I drew that, adding some artistic shading here and there for effect.

As it turned out, Mr. Clark was standing at my elbow when I finished.

"Is that what you saw under the microscope?" he asked. I shrugged. Something in his tone made me know that neither "yea" nor "nay" was the correct answer.

He bent and put his eye to the microscope. After a moment he straightened. "Will, nothing is there."

"But, Mr. Clark, you can see the slide!" I tapped it with my fingernail.

"Indeed. But you forgot to focus properly. Furthermore, the mirror was turned. It was quite dark."

I suppressed a sigh. "Why don't you try again?" His voice was smooth and oiled, like his hair. At that moment I hated him intensely. But if I really meant to convince people that I was a model student, I had to accept any challenge. By the middle of next week, by George, every teacher in Riverton High School was going to trust me—even Harvey Clark. I set to work again.

"And, Will," said Mr. Clark, "remember this is a

biology class, not Renaissance art. You needn't include all the fancy shading this time."

"Yes, sir," I said. "Thank you, sir," and then promptly bit my tongue to keep from saying something I would regret later.

12

THE AFTERNOON WAS HUMID, with temperatures in the 80's. Even so, the downtown area seemed unusually busy for a Friday afternoon. Mother's Day was coming up, but I didn't see how that could account for all the bodies.

The first thing I saw when I walked into Brassey's Book Nook was my mother at the cash drawer, her wispy curls plastered to her forehead and her immaculate white blouse wilted. The shop was overrun with people, some milling about looking, others already with merchandise in hand waiting their turn in the line. I had not seen the place so crowded since Christmas.

Just then Mother looked up and saw me. Relief washed over her face. I made my way to her side through the jumble of customers.

"What're you doing here?" I whispered. "I thought Aunt Jessica wasn't going to Hadley today."

"Oh, William! You can't imagine how glad I am you're here."

"I think I can," I said, "but what's going on?"

She gave me a look that meant I-can't-answer-you-now. I had to be satisfied with that, so I pitched in and helped her make change and add up the amounts of purchase.

All the little pink and blue boxes of stationery disappeared, first from the shelves, then from the window display. The best-selling novel supply became depleted. Bridge cards and scorepads went by the dozens. There did seem to be a lot of chatting and whispering among the customers, but I assumed it was because there were so many of them crammed into the store they couldn't avoid each other.

"Goodness, I don't know *when* I remember Jessica's not being in the store," a woman said to Mother. "Is she . . . ill?"

I turned and looked. The lady, her eyes bright and questioning, was handing Mother a package of party napkins and a dollar bill. Mother took the package and thrust it into a paper sack, put the dollar bill in its proper place, and counted the lady's change into her open palm.

"No," Mother said.

"Well, I'm certainly glad of *that.* Jessica has such a strong constitution. She's truly a remarkable woman, isn't she?"

"Yes," replied Mother.

"Er . . . but I suppose she was terribly upset about Dr. Benson—I mean, since Mrs. Benson is such a good friend of hers?"

"It was a great shock to all of us, as I'm sure it was to you."

"Of course." The lady's voice reflected disappointment. Mother smiled sweetly and turned to the next customer.

Then I understood about the crowds. People were going around trying to pick up bits and scraps of information. They would take the bits home and

124

piece them together, like a quilt, into a pattern that suited them. Curiosity seekers. Gossips. As the realization grew on me, so did anger. If Aunt Jessica were here, I thought, she'd kick 'em all out the door and throw their money after them.

While I was waiting for a little old lady to decide between a red fountain pen and a black one, Lilly walked in. My heart leaped. The sight of her had the effect of making me forget, temporarily, my anger and frustration. I left the old lady crooning over the pens and went to meet Lilly.

"Welcome—a thousand times welcome!" I made a low bow before her that only a week before would have caused her to faint. Now she merely laughed.

"I hardly saw you at school today," she said. "Were you trying to avoid me?"

"Oh, no! I—no." I certainly didn't want her to get *that* idea. "Actually I was trying to . . . stay out of the gossip."

"You *what?*"

"I was trying to avoid the gossiping—the rumor-mongering, or whatever you want to call it, so I—"

"Will Thomas, are you saying that you think I gossip?"

"No! Of course not. I never meant—"

"Well, that's what it sounds like."

"But, Lilly, everyone was talking—you know—about . . ." I lowered my voice to a near whisper, "Dr. Benson and all. *You* know—"

"I know that I don't appreciate being lumped in with the gossips! Someday, Will, when you have the time to spare, you might try to find out what people are really like instead of assuming things about them. Here—you can take this up to the library!"

She thrust a book into my hands, turned on her

125

heel, and walked out. It had all happened so fast, I was left with my mouth open and the book dangling from my hand by its cover.

"Young man, I've made up my mind to get the black one. It's so much more dignified for someone my age, don't you think?" The crackly little-old-lady voice at my elbow grated on my sore feelings like fingernails on slate.

"It's about time!" I snapped, taking the pen and her money.

"What did you say?" She cupped her hand around one ear. "Another dime? Well, let me look in my purse and see if I have another—"

Ah, the perversities of Life, I sighed. "It's all right," I said loudly into her wrinkled ear. "Never mind!"

"Why, thank you! So sweet of you."

The transaction done, the little lady shuffled out. It was exactly five thirty. I closed the door, locked it, and collapsed against it with a loud groan.

"What a mob!"

"Yes, it was, wasn't it?" Mother sounded dazed. She leaned upon one of the counters. "Honestly, I'm trembling from head to toe!"

She held out one hand and I could see that she was, indeed, trembling. I remembered my first day on the job years before, when I had not known prices of things or how to make change. I had been scared to death. I went over and put an arm around her shoulders.

"You were swell. Aunt Jessica herself couldn't have done better."

Mother's eyes were bright and sort of teary. "Do you really mean that? I did want to do well. Jessica was so worried."

"Where is she?"

126

"Let's go sit down. I don't think I can stand up another minute."

We went to the rear of the store. Mother sat in the chair behind Aunt Jessica's desk and I perched on the edge of the desk, telling myself Aunt Jessica would never know.

"I've been here only since noon," Mother said. "Jessica came to the house at eleven. She had been to see Kate Benson, and she was terribly angry at Mr. Nisbett for insisting on an autopsy when Mrs. Benson was so set against it."

"They're not going to find anything," I said obstinately, "except that Dr. Benson died of stinginess."

"William!"

"Well, it's true. What did he ever do for this town?"

"Why, he—he—" Mother tried to think. "He made a lot of money. He *must* have done something."

I let it drop. "Where is Aunt Jessica now?"

"She decided the best thing she could do was to get herself out of financial difficulty so that Kate Benson would not feel responsible and worried during all of this trouble. She caught the noon train to Hadley to see Alva's friend. She expects to return late tonight."

"Well," I said, "we'll have to count today's receipts before we go. You did so well that Aunt Jessica will probably be able to make a payment to the bank, whether she gets the loan or not!"

Mother looked so pleased that I decided not to tell her why all the people happened to be there that day. I figured she knew anyway, whether or not she said so.

Saturday morning when I arrived at work I was already out of sorts about Lilly's being angry at me for no good reason. It did not help that I found Aunt

127

Jessica in a despondent mood. The full money sack and tidings of the previous day's crowd did not cheer her. Yes, she had gone to Hadley, and yes, Alva's friend would pay off the bank. She would pay him back as she could.

"That's swell!" I said. "Mrs. Benson will be glad of that."

Yes, she supposed so.

"What's the matter, Aunt Jessica? Is there something I can do?"

Yes, I could take some money out of my week's wages and go buy my mother a Mother's Day gift, since I probably hadn't given it a thought.

That irritated me, but only because she was right. I hadn't gotten Mother a present and tomorrow, of all days, she needed a boost, with G.C. gone and all. I took some money and went out.

An hour later I came back raging.

"Aunt Jessica, people are saying that Mrs. Benson didn't report the doctor missing Thursday night—on purpose! They keep hinting that she is somehow responsible for his being dead! I can't *believe* this town!"

Aunt Jessica looked grim, but she said nothing.

"It makes me madder than *heck!*" I stormed, flinging my cap halfway across the store. "It isn't true— not a word of it. Dumb, stupid people!"

"I hope that you kept your counsel."

"Yes—I did. But I thought I was going to bust wide open!"

"Burst, William." She turned away from me for a moment, and somehow the defeated slump of her solid shoulders calmed me down. "The next several days are going to be especially difficult. You are going to find it hard not to tell the truth as you know it, but

128

let me impress upon you that you—we—can do Kate the greatest good by *not* telling what we know."

She faced me again. "There may be legal difficulties. If it comes to that, the most reliable witnesses will be those who have not engaged in spreading rumors and gossip."

"Yes, ma'am. I know that."

"Good. Now, go get your cap off that picture frame and let's get to work."

At the First Baptist Church on Sunday morning, the ladies literally swarmed around Aunt Jessica. In the midst of their fluttering pastel presences she was like the dark center of a daisy. Most of them would have enjoyed the role of confidant to a tragic heroine, but Aunt Jessica didn't relish it at all. She made no effort to disguise her disgust.

"How *is* Mrs. Benson?" someone asked.

"Doing as well as could be expected," said Aunt Jessica.

"It was so tragic—and so strange!" said the lady.

Aunt Jessica swallowed air and thrust the point of her umbrella into the earth so viciously that I was sure she wished the ground was actually the ribs or the backside of one of the ladies. However, she did not disgrace either herself or Mrs. Benson by exploding.

I received enlightenment on another matter that day while sitting with Mother and Dad in church. G.C. did not come, although Mother kept looking over her shoulder to see whether he might have slipped in. In a way I felt sorry for her, since on Mother's Day a woman's greatest pride was to have her brood beside her at church. I wondered if G.C. wasn't carrying things too far. His only contact with us since leaving was to send word through the men

129

who came to haul away his boxes and suitcases that he had rented a room with a Mrs. Forbes on Third Street.

Mrs. Hamilton came and sat in the pew behind us. She leaned forward and tapped Mother on the shoulder. "Edith, I just saw G.C. on his way to church—"

Mother's face brightened.

"With Dolores Clammett. She's such a nice girl." Mrs. Hamilton prattled on without seeing that Mother's face had clouded over. "A hard worker. If G.C.'s going to settle down, I can't think of a better girl for him."

It was all I could do not to whoop right out loud. So that was it! G.C. and Dolores wanted to get married, and Mother and Dad couldn't adjust to the idea. I rubbed my mouth to keep from grinning, in deference to the strained look on Mother's face. If G.C. and Dolores got married, that would make Bull and me brothers—sort of.

I made a point of being extra nice to Mother that day, for G.C.'s sake.

Because Dr. Benson was such a famous man, any student who wished to attend his funeral on Monday was excused from classes. A number of us wore our Sunday clothes for the second day in a row and went to swell the ranks of the mourners in St. Bartholomew's Episcopal Church. I went because of Aunt Jessica and Mrs. Benson.

Most of us walked back to school after the funeral was over. I contrived to walk with Lilly.

"Is everything all right?" I asked cautiously.

"Of course. Why shouldn't it be?"

"I hadn't talked to you since Friday, so I wasn't sure."

"Why should you care one way or the other?"

130

I called up all my reserves of politeness, patience, and humility. "I care a lot. I miss talking to you."

"Aren't you afraid I'll tell you some gossip?"

"Lilly, you misunderstood. I wasn't talking about you. I know that you don't gossip. I was only trying to keep *myself* from blabbing. I knew I'd shoot off my mouth whether or not I had anything to say. So I stayed away from everyone Friday. That's the truth."

She looked as though she wanted to forgive me, but didn't really think I was repentant. Then I heard Bull's rough voice muttering a few steps behind us. I stiffened.

"The words of his mouth were smoother than butter," Bull was saying, "but war was in his heart. Psalm fifty-five, verse twenty-one."

I whirled. "O.K., wise guy, what's all that?"

Bull, in his brown Sunday tweeds, looked at me in mock surprise. "I beg your pardon?"

"What kind of junk is that you're spouting?"

"My good man, I was quoting the Holy Scriptures —or didn't you recognize it?"

"What's the big idea, eavesdropping on other people's conversations?"

"I don't know what you mean," Bull said righteously. "I was merely walking along, contemplating aloud. The funeral put me in a solemn mood."

"Well, why don't you just contemplate to yourself? Lilly and I have some important business to tend to." I took her arm and steered her toward the school yard.

"I don't doubt it. Don't forget, Lilly, 'The words of his mouth were smoother than butter—'"

"Awwwwww, shuttup!" I yelled, and practically pushed Lilly across the street and through the base-

131

ment entrance of the school. Bull's laughter followed us. I thought I heard it even when the door closed behind us. To my chagrin, Lilly was laughing too.

"He's not that funny," I said.

"No—but you are. I've never seen you let anyone get the best of you like that."

"He didn't get the best of me!"

"Calm down." She put a hand on my arm. "What important business do we have to tend to?"

She had changed gears so suddenly that it took me a few seconds to get my bearings. I was very conscious of her hand on my arm.

"You said Wednesday you would go with me to see Miss Lauderbach."

She nodded.

"Well, after Friday I was afraid you'd changed your mind."

"No. As a matter of fact, I've already been to Miss Lauderbach and volunteered to help plan the program."

I guess my mouth dropped open. "But—I thought we were going to do that together!"

"Come on," she said. She took my arm and this time I was the one who was steered along, up two flights of stairs to Miss Lauderbach's room. The final class of the day was not yet in session. Lilly led me straight to Miss Lauderbach's desk.

"I've brought another volunteer," she announced. "Will wants to help with the Commencement program, if that's all right with you."

"Why of course, Lilly." Miss Lauderbach's eyebrows climbed slightly. "You're the chairman of that committee, so you can designate anyone with whom you want to work." Her sentence sounded unfinished, as though she might wish to add, "even William Thomas."

"Chairman?" To my embarrassment my voice cracked. "You're the chairman?"

"Yes," said Lilly, "and the committee is meeting tomorrow during lunch period. We'll decide then what needs to be done and divide up the tasks."

"Who?"

"You—Miss Lauderbach—Paul Nisbett—Bull Clammett—and me."

Her calmness dumbfounded me. Miss Lauderbach nodded and smiled approval. I found myself nodding too, although the idea of serving on a committee with Paul and Bull was almost more than I could handle. Still, if it was the only way, I'd just have to do it.

"It's a great relief to have someone take the responsibility, Lilly," Miss Lauderbach was saying. "Perhaps I'm getting old, but I've had so much to think about these past weeks I've hardly been able to sleep. You'll never know how grateful I am that you thought of this."

"Actually," said Lilly, smiling at me, "it was Will's idea."

Oh, Lord! I thought. Don't let Miss Lauderbach think that over! I managed a weak smile. "Not really," I said hastily. "I just mentioned the other day that I thought it would be nice to offer to help. But Lilly doesn't just talk, as you can see. She acts."

"Yes," said Miss Lauderbach. "Thank goodness for those who act."

A bell rang and Lilly looked up at me with an expression that was like a worker dusting his hands together after a job done.

"Time for me to go to home ec," she said. "See you later."

And she was gone. I stumbled down to the basement and biology class, feeling all the while that the horse I had prodded to move had somehow gotten out of my control and was galloping over the plain, dragging me in the traces.

13

BUSINESS AT BRASSEY'S BOOK NOOK was back to normal Monday afternoon, probably because people were worn out from what our Lucille called "all the funeralizing." Aunt Jessica worked downstairs in the store and I stayed in the library. At five thirty she came upstairs. Her footsteps were slow and heavy. Frankly, I was worried about her. The recent trouble had seemed to take the starch out of her, and Aunt Jessica without starch was hardly Aunt Jessica at all. Not even the news that Dr. Benson had died of simple heart failure brought on by physical exertion could make her feel better. It had also been established that the satchel he was holding when the constable found him had not contained anything of value. He had not been robbed. I knew a lot of people would be secretly disappointed.

"I feel that I should go by to see Kate before going home, William. Would you like to come with me?"

No, I thought, but I didn't say that. "I'll go if you want me to."

If she caught the reluctance in my tone, she didn't let on. "That would be very good of you," she said. And so, after turning out lights and locking up, we walked along Main Street in the late afternoon. Aunt

Jessica had little to say. For the first time I became aware that I was taller than she. I could look over the crown of her black straw hat. Funny I hadn't noticed that before. I had taken for granted that Aunt Jessica would always be the taller. Now some mysterious reversal had taken place. I knew that from this time, while I grew taller and stronger, she would seem to grow smaller and more fragile. Knowing made me both sad and anxious.

We turned at Hildebrande. The collective shade of the arching maples rushed toward us in a cool breath. Aunt Jessica was out of place on this street in her black crepe that was shiny and worn. The heels of her substantial shoes thumped upon the pavement. And yet walking beside her was still like accompanying an ocean liner. Hildebrande Avenue would have to accommodate to her, instead of the other way around.

We came to the Bensons' iron gate, and as usual I was intimidated by it. A few cars were parked in the street in front and some in the driveway. Not all the mourners had departed. I wanted to pluck at Aunt Jessica's sleeve and ask if we might come back another day. The naked fountain boy threw water in our direction. Aunt Jessica hardly noticed. She drew the gate latch and went in, with me following close in her wake. As she moved up the flagstone walk I couldn't help wondering whether somewhere in the core of her being she felt as uneasy as I did, but if she did, she didn't show it.

We went up on the porch and she rang the bell. Immediately the door opened and the stuffy butler stood there peering down at us. She took from her black purse an engraved card.

"Would you please tell Mrs. Benson that Mrs.

Brassey is here and would like to see her if she feels like receiving callers."

The butler took the card delicately between index finger and thumb. "Mrs. Benson," he began, and then because he made the mistake of looking Aunt Jessica in the eye, his voice trailed off. "Please come in while I see . . ."

We followed him into the house. There were other people in the rooms we passed, but it was all impersonal, like a hotel lobby. The draperies were drawn. The air smelled of too many flowers. The butler showed us into Dr. Benson's library. While we waited my eyes roved over the heavy, elegant furniture, the rich carpeting, the *objets d'art,* the volumes and volumes of books. I had not known such things existed in Riverton. Not even my afternoon lemonade in the front parlor had prepared me for this.

Shortly we heard soft footsteps in the hall and Mrs. Benson entered. Against the dark furnishings of the room she was like a gray mist, hardly substantial. I stood up as she came in, but she went straight to Aunt Jessica. Both of them cried. I did not like to watch. After a while Mrs. Benson turned to me and took my hand briefly, and then we all sat down. I wished I were in New York or the Sahara Desert or somewhere. I hoped no one expected me to say anything.

Aunt Jessica and Mrs. Benson talked quietly about the funeral and who was there and such. Then Aunt Jessica said, "You know I should like to have been with you these two days, but you must know, too, why I have stayed away."

Mrs. Benson's eyes filled and she nodded.

"One thing I must tell you is that I have been to see a friend of Alva's in Hadley, and he has taken over my payments to the bank. You are not to worry any more about *that.*"

"Oh, but Jess—"

Aunt Jessica held up a firm hand. "You ought to know me well enough to realize I'm being perfectly honest. Put it out of your mind."

"Very well, then. For the time being."

There was a long pause, then Aunt Jessica asked whether Mrs. Benson had someone to attend to her legal affairs.

"Yes," Mrs. Benson said. "Since Paul is Edgar's only kin he is taking care of that for me. I was so relieved that he would attend to it."

My ears twitched. At first I thought she meant my classmate, Paul, but then realized she was talking about his father. Aunt Jessica looked at her sharply as if she had questions about that. But if she did, she kept them to herself. She nodded and said that was fine and stood up to go. I did too, glad that we weren't going to stay any longer.

"You can call me at any hour of the day or night," she said to Mrs. Benson. "Please feel free to do that."

"Yes, I know. In a strange place it is good to have a true friend like you, Jess. Thank you."

Her words echoed in my head as we went out behind the butler. Did Mrs. Benson really feel like a stranger, even though she had lived in Riverton all these years? Aunt Jessica and I walked in silence down the flagstone path, through the gate, and to the sidewalk. Ordinarily we would have parted ways, but I didn't want to leave her for some reason.

"I'll walk home with you," I said.

"Very well. I shall be glad of your company."

We walked for a while without talking. I was sad and did not know why. The breezes stirred the leaves

138

and I thought of ghosts whispering, of changes occurring, of growing old and dying alone. I kept thinking of Mrs. Benson.

"How will things be for her now, Aunt Jessica?"

"Well, I suppose after the estate is settled she will be comfortably fixed at last—and will have freedom to spend money for those things that are truly important to her."

"Is it a lot of money?"

"Nearly a million dollars."

I couldn't even think how much money that was, or how one could possibly think of ways to spend it.

"At least she can pay you back now," I said.

"I'd be happy if she never thought of that money again," Aunt Jessica replied, and I knew that it was true.

We reached her house and she invited me in, but I declined. "I have to be home for dinner," I said. "G.C. isn't there anymore, you know."

"That's true. And in another year or so, you won't be there either. Poor Edith. I don't think she is quite ready for that."

"Well," I said, "Mother did a fine job at the store Friday. If you ever think of hiring someone in my place, I wish you'd consider her for the position."

"Thank you for the recommendation. I trust your judgment."

Then to my surprise she leaned over and gave me a quick kiss on the cheek. "Good night, William. Keep your ears open and your mouth closed."

And she went inside. I walked home thinking how odd it was that an aunt could be a friend as well as a relative.

Next day at lunch period we assembled in Miss Lauderbach's room for our first committee meeting.

It was a motley group—Paul, Bull, Lilly, Miss Lauderbach, and I. Miss Lauderbach beamed, a disconcert-
ing sight in itself. Bull's tongue poked a lump in his
cheek as he looked at me with knowing eyes. I looked
at the ceiling a lot. Paul, eager as usual, sat forward
in his chair so as not to miss a single word.

Lilly stood up. "There are a lot of things to be done
during the next two weeks, so I'm going to give each
of you an assignment. Call on anyone in the junior
class to help you—the more people you involve, the
better.

"Paul, you're in charge of stage decorations—
flowers, bunting, a banner for the class of '23, and so
forth."

Paul was delighted. He wrote something on a piece
of paper. I stifled a snort.

"Bull, you and Will are to work together on the
decorations and refreshments for the reception for
the graduates. It will be in the school cafeteria and
we expect three hundred people to attend. I'd suggest that one of you be in charge of decorations and
the other of refreshments."

There was, as they say, a pregnant pause while Bull
and I regarded each other. It was a put-up job. Lilly
knew we were not on speaking terms, so what the
heck did she think she was doing? I waited for Bull
to say, "Nothing doing. I wouldn't work with that
Blankety for a million bucks!"

But he didn't say it. He just sat there and so did I.
Lilly took our silence as assent, I could see.

"Refreshments is a girl's job," I said.

"Then get some girls to help you," Lilly shot back.
"I'm going to get the awards and medals boxed and
wrapped for presentation."

"Hey, no fair!" I protested. "No one's supposed to
140

know who gets the awards before they're given out."

"Don't worry about that," said Miss Lauderbach. "Lilly will not know who is going to receive the awards. She will only be responsible for getting them ready."

"Oh. Well—in that case, if you need boxes and wrapping paper you can get them at Aunt Jessica's bookstore. She might even donate them."

"That's a good suggestion!" Lilly wrote something in her notebook. "I'll see Mrs. Brassey this very afternoon."

I avoided looking at Bull.

"If there are no more questions, we'll adjourn," Lilly said. "Remember, I'm the person you should bother if you have problems. If I can't handle them, I'll go to Miss Lauderbach, but we'll try very hard not to worry her with details." Miss Lauderbach smiled and smiled.

"And," said Lilly, "I'd advise you to get right to work. There isn't much time."

The bell rang for afternoon classes to begin. As we started out Bull fell into step beside me. "I didn't know *you* were going to be on this thing or I never would have volunteered," he said.

"Same here. You can always pull out, you know."

"Who, me? You think I'm going to let you take over? You're crazy! Why don't *you* pull out?"

I shook my head. "I've been waiting for this chance ever since the day you told me who was going to win the history medal. Everything's falling into place at last. I can't fight Fate, can I?"

"No," said Bull, giving me a funny look. "I guess you can't, at that." He turned into a classroom and left me standing in the hall.

14

FOR NEARLY A WEEK my life went so smoothly that I began to be uneasy. Mother and Dad had adjusted more quickly than I thought they would to G.C.'s departure. Besides, he was being seen so much and so openly with Dolores Clammett that they were beginning to accept that part of his life almost in spite of themselves.

Our meals at home, instead of being quiet and morose, took a turn. Mother became downright chatty, to Dad's puzzlement. Once she brought up the subject of getting a job—*not*, she said hastily, because Dad hadn't provided adequately for us, but because she had enjoyed her day at the bookstore so very much. Dad tried to discourage her by saying that she would be tired of it by the end of a week. But instead of giving in, Mother argued that of course she would get tired of it, just as she got tired of doing housework and cooking day in and day out, but that didn't mean she would quit, for goodness' sakes! Anything worth doing, she said, was going to be demanding, and there would always be times when you wanted to quit doing it. For instance, she went on, pointing at me, William here must get terribly tired of school, but there's no question of his quitting—is there, William?

I shook my head, overwhelmed by the suddenness of the question.

"Well," said Dad, "I hope you won't make a hasty decision. You don't have to work."

"If William goes to college—" she began, and then decided not to pursue the subject. The words hung in the air, unfinished.

I thought about them in the days that followed. *If* William goes to college. If *William* goes to college. If William goes to *college.* It was a question with many shades and inferences. The awful truth was that I hadn't given much practical consideration to my life beyond Riverton High School. It was mostly daydreams, which I began to realize had very little of the stamp of reality upon them. Being a general in the Foreign Legion or a star of Hollywood film or U.S. Senator from North Carolina was not a circumstance one usually fell into at the age of seventeen.

Perhaps it was the weight of these matters that subdued me and made me more cooperative than I might otherwise have been. I worked with Bull on my part of the Commencement activities and we steered away from subjects that focused on our conflict. He knew that I was up to something that had to do with Paul, but he didn't ask me what it was.

Lilly did amazing things. She even finagled boxes and wrapping paper from Aunt Jessica with such finesse that Aunt Jessica was impressed. My basic problem was, as usual, Paul Nisbett, but for different reasons from formerly. My feelings of enmity were no longer clear-cut. I wanted desperately to find his weak spot. Somewhere beneath that flawless exterior

143

there had to be a blemish, a flaw. Finally, though, I had to concede that he really was what he appeared to be—a decent, guileless, earnest, eager beaver. If he had a flaw, it was only that he wanted to please everyone. That irritated me. It was so opposite from me.

I hardly left Lilly's side, and she came to rely on me as her first lieutenant. I fell into the pattern of maintaining my good behavior everywhere. I turned in all homework on time. I did extra work that was not required. I listened—or pretended to—in class. I did not copy anyone else's paper. I arrived at English class five minutes before the first bell. I deferred to teachers' decisions. Where formerly I could smell any mischief brewing—that is, if I hadn't begun it myself—now I shied away from any activity that even hinted at mutiny or dissent.

There was a marked change in other people's attitudes toward me. The teachers gave me all sorts of responsibilities. I ran messages to the principal's office. I counted money that students turned in. I was allowed to leave classes on my own cognizance. At home Mother no longer hounded me to get up in the morning. Dad did not require an accounting if I happened to arrive for dinner a few minutes late.

It was a strange feeling to be trusted. Part of me liked it. But part of me laughed wildly at the tremendous joke I was putting over on them all. They thought I had reformed! Nobody asked anymore what I was up to.

But while the externals of my life had changed radically, inside Brassey's Book Nook and the Riverton Public Library, things were the same as they had always been.

"Have you noticed a change in me?" I asked Aunt

144

Jessica point-blank one afternoon.

She put her head to one side and studied me seriously. Then she said, "No."

"None at all? Don't you think I'm—er—more responsible? Getting more work done? Things like that?"

"No." She seemed genuinely puzzled by my question. "You've always been responsible and hardworking." And she turned back to her own work, leaving me to ponder her reply.

The week of graduation was upon us at last. I came to work Monday afternoon to find Aunt Jessica near tears. The newspaper had just arrived. She had spread it out upon her desk and was shaking her head in despair. The headline read: BENSON WILL TO BE CONTESTED BY RELATIVES.

"Whew!" I whistled, staring at the tall black letters. "What happened?"

"Read it for yourself," she said, thrusting the paper at me.

It was learned today that Paul Nisbett, Sr., owner and operator of Riverton Cotton Gin, has entered suit in Superior Court contesting the will of Dr. Edgar Benson, who died on May 11. The will, as read on Tuesday last, named Mrs. Katherine Benson, widow of the deceased doctor, heir to his money, property, and shares of stock. Mr. Nisbett, a cousin of Dr. Benson, has entered the suit on behalf of himself and his own heirs, claiming that the doctor had not intended to exclude his kinsmen from the will. The suit contends that the will was written and witnessed during the final months of the doctor's life when he was not of sound mind. The caveators will seek to prove that the doctor was not competent to make a will.

Mrs. Benson could not be reached for comment when this paper went to press.

I read it through once, and then once again. "I don't get it. I thought a will was a will. I mean, if Dr. Benson wanted to leave his money to Mrs. Benson, why should Mr. Nisbett try to horn in? He's already got more money than he can spend anyhow!"

"Yes," she said, "but the prospect of more is too enticing for most people to resist, especially if they feel it is rightfully theirs. Mr. Nisbett wants the money, but doesn't need it—although I daresay he would disagree with that statement. Kate needs the money."

"But," I argued, "nobody needs *that* much money —not even Mrs. Benson."

"That's true. Kate would be the first to say so. The disturbing thing is that while she would be fair and generous with her money after her own needs were met, I'm not sure that Mr. Nisbett would."

I looked at the newspaper again. "You notice what it says about Mr. Nisbett's heirs? He doesn't have but *one* heir—old Goody Two-shoes—"

Aunt Jessica gave me a sharp look. "I'm sure Paul, Jr., can't help what his father does any more than you can help what yours does."

That stung. I didn't like her taking up for Paul. She didn't know him that well. "I'm sure he's not kicking about it," I said. "After all, look what he'll get if his dad wins the suit."

She did not reply to that. Instead she took the paper from me, folded it, and laid it upon her desk. "They will be looking for testimony from anyone who was with Dr. Benson when he was acting strangely."

We looked at each other. I had a sinking feeling. "I don't feel so good."

"Nor I. The pity of it is that I agree that Edgar

146

Benson was dotty—eccentric—whatever you want to call it. But I don't agree that he was incompetent when he made his will in Kate's favor. So far as I'm concerned, it's the only right-minded thing he did."

Brassey's Book Nook was not a place of good cheer for the remainder of the afternoon. Aunt Jessica was glum. I proposed that she tend the library and let me handle the store, since she didn't feel like smiling. She didn't even argue.

Business was slow. A few people came and went, but there were long empty periods between. The window display that had been so depleted on the day of Dr. Benson's death still had not been refurbished. Without consulting Aunt Jessica I decided to fix it myself. I got a clean rag and the window cleaner to wipe the fingerprints from the sidewalk side of the glass. But instead of thinking about the display, I thought about the Benson will and about Mrs. Benson's problems. It seemed to me there must be some way to keep the machinery of a legal suit from getting under way, if only I could think it through.

"Look, you dummy," I said to my reflection in the glass, "you created the problems in the first place by interfering in something that was none of your business. If you'd stayed out of it, Dr. Benson might still be alive right now!"

My hand dropped to my side and I stared, horrified, at my reflected self. Had I said that?

Feeling slightly ill, I went back inside the store and sat down in the chair behind Aunt Jessica's cluttered desk.

If only I had kept my mouth shut. If only Aunt Jessica had told me at the beginning that she had lent Mrs. Benson money . . . and why. If only—

I hit the desk with my fist. The biggest "if only"

147

was If Only I would consider the consequences to other people before I did some stupid thing.

I don't know how long I sat there. If someone had come along, picked me up, and stuffed me into a dark closet, I don't think I would have put up a struggle. I might, in fact, have welcomed the excuse to withdraw from the human race.

"William!"

Aunt Jessica's voice coming from upstairs sounded like the voice of a harsh ghost. I let her call twice before I answered.

"If you don't have anything else to do, I wish you'd be thinking about something to put in the window!"

"Yes, ma'am." I heaved myself out of the chair, picked up the cleaning rag, and went back out to the sidewalk.

15

MOTHER AND DAD were talking about the suit when I got home from work. Unlike former times, they did not stop when I walked in, but went right on with their conversation. I flopped down on the divan and closed my eyes.

"Mr. Nisbett never so much as hinted to me that he had such a thing in mind," Dad was saying.

"Well," said Mother, "I suppose he was afraid to mention it, for fear you would try to discourage him. It seems to me that the very least he could do would be to tell you what he was about instead of letting you read it in the newspaper."

"Yes, I suppose so. But of course it really has nothing to do with me."

They sat in silence for a few moments, then Mother said timidly, "I still don't understand why Mr. Nisbett feels he must lay claim to the money. Didn't Dr. Benson leave him anything?"

"Ten thousand dollars, I believe," replied Dad.

I rolled over on my side and stared at him. "Golly! Ten thousand dollars? Then why is he contesting the will? Ten thousand dollars—wow!"

"Because," said Dad patiently, "ten thousand dollars is a mere fraction of the total amount of money.

Mr. Nisbett feels he's entitled to more than that."

"But what did he ever do for Dr. Benson?"

"Who knows? That isn't the issue."

"I wonder how Mrs. Benson feels about all this," I said. "She must be furious."

"No, I just imagine she's very sad," Dad commented. "If she loses, she won't be destitute. State law provides that she will get a handsome settlement. But just think of all the dirty linen that Mr. Nisbett will have to air in order to win!"

"What would happen," I asked, "if Aunt Jessica testified that she had to lend money to Mrs. Benson so the servants could be paid?"

"Number one—that fact would serve to prove that Dr. Benson really wasn't quite rational about his money. Number two, it might win some sympathy for Mrs. Benson, but it would cast Jessica in a bad light. It could be said that she was trying to ingratiate herself with Mrs. Benson in hopes of getting some favor in return."

"Well!" Mother said so fervently and unexpectedly that Dad and I both looked at her in astonishment. "It just makes me thankful we're not rich and prominent!"

"That's certainly a change of tune," I said.

"I don't know what you mean," said Mother.

"G.C. and Dolores would," I answered.

It was the first time I had mentioned their names together in the same sentence in the presence of my parents. Mother's mouth tightened as it usually did when the subject was brought up.

"I'm sure Dolores is a very nice girl," she said. "She's just not the person I would have chosen for him."

150

"Who would you have chosen?"

"I—well, someone who would have . . . who would lift him up."

"Up from what?"

"Well, you know what I mean! Up from . . . his circumstances. Someone who would encourage him to better himself. He's so contented in that hardware store, and her working there doesn't help the situation!"

"But, Mother, G.C. will probably own that store someday! Isn't that true, Dad?"

Mother looked first at me and then at Dad. "What?"

"Mr. Marcus doesn't have a son to carry on. G.C. will probably be his partner before long, and then eventually buy out the business. Surely you know that!"

Dad cleared his throat. "We don't know that at all, William, and I don't—"

"Haven't you ever been to see G.C. work? Why, he knows more about what's in that store than Mr. Marcus does. He does the buying, he writes the ads for the paper—the whole thing!"

"William, G.C. is a hard worker, but frankly, he has never had the potential for success that, say, *you* have . . . or Paul Nisbett."

I was furious. "No wonder he moved out! What do you call success anyway? What's better than doing what you like to do and making a decent living at it?"

There is no telling what I might have said next, but the phone rang and Dad sent me to answer it. Out in the hallway I let it ring a couple of times before answering to give myself time to simmer down. It occurred to me then that in spite of all my arguing,

Dad hadn't made me go to my room. During the past week or so, I had crossed some mysterious border without knowing it.

The phone call was from Lilly. She was trying to get the committee together at her house at eight to go over last-minute details. Could I come?

Could I! I wanted to get out of the house, away from thinking about the trial or about family problems.

Lilly met me at the door dressed in a new pink outfit and I regretted right away that this was a committee meeting. Bull and Paul had already arrived.

"Now," said Lilly brightly, when she had ushered me into the living room, "you can entertain each other while I get popcorn and lemonade." She left, and the living room closed in upon us. The strained relations between Bull and me accounted for part of the problem. Besides that, though, Paul seemed very subdued. I wondered if he was embarrassed at what his father had done—or did he even care? The prospect of falling heir to nearly a million dollars could make a person indifferent to a lot of things, including the good opinion of his peers.

When our hostess came back, we seized upon her presence as drowning men grab at flotsam. She put the popcorn and lemonade on a table in our midst and we covered our unease by stuffing and guzzling.

According to each report, everything was going smoothly. Paul had a crew working on the auditorium decorations. Bull and I were to be excused from classes the last two days of school in order to decorate the cafeteria. The refreshment committee was under orders to produce enough cookies and punch to feed a small battalion. It was all sewed up. No doubt Miss

Lauderbach pinched herself three times a day to be sure she wasn't dreaming.

"And I have something to show you." Lilly went out and returned with a large cardboard box which she set on the floor at our feet. She pulled back the flaps. "Here are the awards, all wrapped and ready to go."

The large box was full of a number of smaller boxes, many shapes and varied sizes. I recognized the paper they were wrapped with as some Aunt Jessica kept in stock.

"Gee, I didn't realize they gave out *that* many awards at Commencement," Bull said.

"I didn't either until I started working on them," said Lilly. "But you realize they aren't just for seniors." She took out several, reading from a list she had pasted at the top of the box.

My mouth was dry. "How . . . can you tell which one is which, now that they're all wrapped?"

"They're numbered. The number on the list corresponds to the one on the box. Miss Lauderbach will match numbers and names on Commencement night."

"You did a nice job of wrapping those," I said. I longed to see the list. Which of those boxes contained the history medal?

"Oh, well. I wanted you to see that I hadn't just been giving orders and not doing any work myself." Lilly began putting the smaller boxes back into the cardboard box.

I leaped from the rocking chair and got down on my knees beside her. "Here—let me help."

But she grabbed my hand before I could touch anything. "No. I'd better do it. They have to go back in a particular order so the person who hands out the awards won't have to scramble for each one, or get them mixed up."

I felt like a kid whose hands have been slapped for reaching across the table.

"But it was nice of you to offer," Bull whispered at my back. No one else heard him. My ears burned.

I needed to look at the list, but Lilly was already picking up the box.

"Wait!" I said. "I know you're strong and all that, but it's embarrassing for you to be carrying that box when there are three able-bodied males around. I *insist* that you let me carry it."

"All right." Lilly shrugged. "Take it and follow me."

With the box in my arms and the list directly under my eyes, I found what I wanted to know. "Douglas History Medal. Number 22."

The box went into the coat closet in the hall. So now I knew which number, but I hadn't seen the box that contained the medal—I didn't know its size and shape or how it was wrapped. But I intended to find out. Then I would duplicate the box and wrappings and make a switch before Friday night. Paul Nisbett would think he was getting the Douglas History Medal, but . . .

It was all I could do not to break into a loud yell, to leap and knock my heels together. Instead I smiled at Lilly—which made her blush—and followed her back to the living room.

Bull left shortly, and I kept waiting for Paul to do the same so that I would have some time with Lilly, but it became obvious that he wasn't going to leave until I did. I finally gave up. We left together, and from the satisfied look on Lilly's face when she told us good night, you would think she had planned it that way.

We walked along for a while without saying much of anything. I couldn't think of anything to talk about.

"Will," he said suddenly, "why don't you like me?"

The question bowled me over. It was about the last thing I expected.

"I . . . don't know that it's a case of not liking you," I hedged. "I don't know you very well, that's all."

"I suppose I've had the feeling you didn't really care to. I thought maybe I'd done something to make you angry."

Nothing but outdo me in everything I undertake. Nothing but be rich as hell and not have to worry about your future. Nothing but be every teacher's favorite student.

"Naw," I said. "I don't know of anything."

"I don't want to be your enemy."

"You're not my enemy." I did not know whether I lied. I had a knot in my stomach. I started walking faster.

"You're the most interesting person in our class," Paul said. "I've always admired the way you do what you want to do, without worrying about what someone's going to think."

"How do you know I don't worry about that?" I said gruffly. "You can't always go by appearances."

"I suppose not." He was silent a moment, then said, "Every time I start to do something, I find myself wondering whether Father would approve. I'm always afraid I'll do something to disappoint him."

"I know something about *that,*" I said. "My folks expect a lot of me, too, but they've been disappointed most of my life!"

"But at least when you don't succeed the world doesn't come to an end!"

"No, it doesn't. Which is probably a good thing, since it would be coming to an end at least three times a day, seven days a week. I slip up a lot."

"What happens when you and your father disagree?"

"Nothing much. We argue—he blows his top, and I have to go to my room, or some such. But he hasn't done that much, lately."

"Does he hold the family name and reputation over your head?"

I had to laugh at that. "The Thomases don't *have* a name and reputation. Insignificance is one of the advantages of low estate. You can't go anywhere but up!"

We had reached the corner of Felker and Robbins. Just before we parted ways Paul said, "Does your father ever do anything that you think is wrong?"

"Sure—all the time. He's a stuffed shirt."

"No—I mean *wrong*—against principles."

"Who, my dad? Good Lord, no. He's as righteous as Job!"

Paul didn't respond to that, and I was thinking by that time that this was undoubtedly the strangest conversation I had ever had with anyone. It made me uneasy. He said good night and walked away down Robbins Street. I walked home slowly, pondering what he had said. What was behind all his questions? I thought about Dad—stuffy, pompous, and rigid sometimes, but one thing you could say about him,

156

he lived up to his principles. Oh, my, did he! There was no disparity between what he said and what he did. He was very like Aunt Jessica in that respect. Maybe that's why I had turned out like I did. Too much righteousness in a family can lead to an imbalance.

16

I STAYED AWAKE most of the night staring into the darkness, trying to figure a way to see the box containing the history medal. I only needed to see it once. I could make the switch on the last day, after the awards had been taken to the auditorium. Toward morning I slept, sure that I had at last figured all the angles.

Dad had gone to work when I came down to breakfast. Mother drank her coffee while I ate, looking at me thoughtfully over the rim of her china cup. She seemed much calmer than usual.

"Your father and I had a long talk after you left last night," she said.

"Oh?" I braced myself for more chastisement.

"You know, we may have been too hard on G.C. all these years. I suppose because he was a bit slow in school we naturally assumed he was like that in other things."

"Not everyone is cut out to be a scholar," I said. "Good grades aren't everything."

"Well," she said, *"some* people would use that as an excuse to keep from doing their best."

"Not G.C."

"No, not G.C. I—we've decided to ask him and

158

Dolores to come for Sunday dinner."

I did look at her then. Her mouth was not tight as it usually was when she spoke Dolores' name. I was glad, and I told her so, which seemed to please her very much. She reached into her apron pocket and pulled out a small object, holding it out in the palm of her hand for me to see.

"Look. I found this yesterday while I was cleaning in G.C.'s room. It's his old Sunday school attendance pin, from 1918. I'm going to give it to him Sunday if he comes."

I took the pin and looked at it. It wasn't very large. The writing was in gold letters on red: "Perfect Attendance. Sunday School. 1918." It was exactly what I had been looking for.

"Could I have this?" I asked.

"Oh, I don't think so. It was G.C.'s. He might want to keep it—"

"I don't know about that," I said. "He probably would be embarrassed if you gave it to him now. He'd say you were being sentimental."

"Do you really think so?"

"Yes—so why don't you let me keep it for now, as a kind of memento? One of these days when he and Dolores have a bunch of kids, he'll want it back."

Mother's eyes lighted up when I mentioned kids. "I expect you're right, at that. It would be better to save it for the grandchildren, wouldn't it?" I knew G.C. and Dolores wouldn't have any trouble from her now about getting married. She was already thinking ahead to a new set of children and beginning again as a grandmother.

Before leaving for school I ran up to my room and put the attendance pin in my sock drawer. When Paul opened the award Friday night he would see:

159

Perfect Attendance

Sunday School

1918

I couldn't wait to see the expression on his face. What a gag!

That mental picture buoyed me through the day. I felt jovial and kindly. I was nice to Paul. I sailed through my year-end exams with ease. I hummed a lot.

I also asked Lilly if she'd let me come over that night to study with her. She didn't even act surprised.

"Sure. Come over at eight," was all she said. I wondered how she would act if she knew I was more interested in the cardboard box in her coat closet than I was in either her or the Spanish-American War.

At work I cut off an adequate piece of paper like that Lilly had used to wrap the boxes, folded it, and stuck it in my back pocket. Then I took a yard of the red ribbon. Tomorrow, after I knew the size and shape, I would filch a box. When I got through, not even an expert would be able to tell which was the original and which was the substitute.

That evening at Lilly's I studied history. I learned more about the Spanish-American War than I wanted to know. Finally, after two hours, I said the words I had been rehearsing all day. "I'd like to see the list of awards again."

"Really? Whatever for?"

"Well, I wouldn't tell this to just everyone," I said, looking away, "but I'm already thinking ahead to next year. Now that I've reformed, I ought to aspire to something more than a diploma, don't you think? I'd like to be working for some of those awards."

"That's very ambitious of you."

"I don't know about that. It's none too soon, as far as my parents are concerned."

So we fetched the box out of the hall closet, took it to the living room, and looked at the list pasted on the lid.

"You know," I said, "I bet I can guess who's going to win most of them this year."

"Oh?"

"Yeah. Paul Nisbett." I laughed heartily, but she didn't join me, just studied me in a way that made me decide to calm down.

"Are all the boxes the same size?" I asked.

"Oh, no. Some are little square boxes. Some are long. I'll show you." She opened the box and took out several, to show me. None of them was number 22. I was perspiring.

"You know, I figured that history medal was some huge thing, the way Miss Lauderbach has talked about it," I said casually. "I guess it's not, though, huh?"

She reached into the box and came up with a package that was square and about as large as the palm of my hand minus fingers. Brassey's Book Nook had dozens of boxes that size.

"It's a different sort of medal from the rest—that's true," Lilly said.

"You've seen it, then?"

She nodded. She began putting everything away. I had found out what I wanted to know, but I had to feign an interest in the other awards. I picked out two or three at random that I said I thought I'd like to try to win the next year. Lilly was encouraging. She smiled at me a lot, and I liked it so much I found myself saying things to impress her. I got carried away. Her father came and stuck his head in the door to announce that it was eleven o'clock.

I walked home with my feet scarcely touching the ground.

After that things seemed to move without a hitch. I found a box at the store the next day, and when I got through wrapping the 1918 Sunday school pin, not even Lilly could have told the difference between it and the real medal. I started to put it in my sock drawer, but then I remembered that Mother frequently put away my clean clothes. I finally stuck it between the mattress and springs of G.C.'s bed.

Thursday, Bull and I didn't go to classes at all, but stayed in the cafeteria hanging crepe paper from the rafters. On Friday, the big day, we worked all morning and then went our separate ways home to lunch. While I was home I got the box out of G.C.'s room and stuck it under my shirt just above my belt. I intended to make the switch that afternoon after everyone left school. I had heard Lilly say she was going to take the box of awards to the auditorium sometime that day.

It was only a little after noon when I finished eating, and since I didn't have to be back at the cafeteria before half past one, I decided to drop by the store to let Aunt Jessica know I might not get to work that afternoon. The door was open and the ceiling fans were running, but I saw no sign of Aunt Jessica in the bookstore. Thinking she was probably in the library, I took the steps two at a time, whistling the school alma mater, Dixieland style.

She was in the library, all right, with Mrs. Benson.

It was the first time I had seen Mrs. Benson since the day I had visited her with Aunt Jessica. She had grown old in the past few days. Her face had crumpled like tissue paper. The black mourning did not become her as the gray dresses had done. Aunt Jessica was looking at her with undisguised concern.

"Hello, Mrs. Benson. How are you?" It was a stupid question, but I didn't know what else to say. My arms hung long at my sides.

"Fine, thank you, William. Have you been well?"

"Yes, ma'am. Busy. Graduation tonight, you know."

"But you aren't graduating, are you?"

"No. Next year, if I'm lucky." I told her what the juniors had been doing. She listened as though she didn't want to miss a word.

"I did so enjoy that sort of thing when I taught school," she said. "It was exciting every year."

"You should come tonight—" I began, and then stopped. Paul was her cousin by marriage. Somehow I didn't want Mrs. Benson to witness his Mortifying Moment. She might not think it was funny. "On second thought, it would probably bore you to tears—goes on for hours, you know."

"Well, thank you anyway, but I'm leaving early in the morning," she said, looking down at her gloved hands folded in her lap.

"She's leaving on the train for California," said Aunt Jessica. "For good."

"What? But—how can you do that? I mean, with the tri—"

I bit off the word before it came all the way out, but she knew what I was about to say.

"There won't be a trial, William," said Mrs. Benson.

I looked at Aunt Jessica and saw the message in her eyes that I shouldn't ask any more questions. But I couldn't just walk away.

"Mrs. Benson, I don't want you to go." That was true. I hoped she would know I wasn't just being polite.

"Thank you, William. That's very sweet of you." She stood up and smoothed her black dress. "Perhaps I shall write to you, when I have settled down in California."

I stayed in the library while Aunt Jessica went down with her. All sorts of questions were going through my head. It seemed to me that the only way Mrs. Benson could leave now was simply to hand over every cent to Mr. Nisbett. I didn't see how she could do that, but when Aunt Jessica returned in a few minutes, I learned that was exactly what she intended to do. I had never seen my aunt in such despair.

"It's so needless!" she kept saying,, pacing up and down the library until the floor squeaked. "If Paul Nisbett knew what she was doing—"

Suddenly she stopped pacing, turned, and faced me.

"Of course," she said, as though she had just received enlightenment. "It's the only thing to do."

I could only look at her dumbly.

17

"I WANT YOU to accompany me, William."

"Aunt Jessica, you shouldn't—"

"I should, and I shall. Now—will you go with me or not?"

"People will be surprised," I said. "It's not two o'clock yet. Wouldn't you rather I stayed here and kept the shop open?"

"I want you with me." She was adamant. I could not for the life of me understand why she wanted me along, but I stifled a sigh and went around turning off lights. Aunt Jessica drew the shade on the front door, hung up the CLOSED sign, and, as we departed, locked the door.

It was a hot afternoon, but she hardly seemed to notice the weather. She moved along the sidewalk with her accustomed vigor, her blue eyes full of purpose, her umbrella pacing her with brisk little clicking noises as she set it down, picked it up, set it down.

"Supposing Mr. Nisbett isn't there?" I said, panting slightly with the effort of keeping up with her.

"I shall worry about that if and when."

"Wouldn't it be more businesslike to make an appointment with him?"

"There's no time for that. This is Friday. Kate intends to leave tomorrow."

"Aunt Jessica, please don't do anything crazy! It will only make things worse. Believe me, I know!"

We had come to the end of the sidewalk and were about to cross the street. Aunt Jessica turned and looked at me squarely. "William, one thing you must remember—there's a difference between doing something crazy just to get attention and doing something crazy for the sake of someone you care about."

The traffic light turned green and we crossed the street.

"How do you know it'll do any good?"

"William, you can be so exasperating! I *don't* know, but the way things are now, Kate has nothing. How can she lose Nothing?"

My mind would not receive this complicated bit of logic. I quit arguing and resigned myself to the adventure. Under my shirt the corners of the award box dug into my skin.

When we arrived in the Gin yard, she paused long enough to consult her watch and to wipe the perspiration from her face with her handkerchief. Then closing her purse with a loud snap and lifting her chin, she marched up the steps to the wooden porch and walked into the office.

Mrs. Preston was startled, not to say shaken. Aunt Jessica on these premises was as unusual a sight, say, as a whale in a garden pool. She rose quickly and came round to confront us. The smile on her lips went no farther than that. Her eyes looked worried.

"Good afternoon, Mrs. Brassey. How nice to see you!"

I thought she spoke rather too loudly, and then realized she wanted both Dad and Mr. Nisbett to

166

hear. Dad got the message first. He appeared at his office door in time to hear Aunt Jessica say, "Good afternoon, Flora. I should like to speak to Mr. Nisbett, if you please."

Mrs. Preston's smile remained fixed. Her white hands joined nervously just at waist level. "I see. Do you have an appointment?"

"You are his secretary, are you not?"

"Why, yes, I—"

"Then you should know perfectly well that I don't have an appointment. However, this is a matter of extreme urgency."

While Mrs. Preston cast about for something to say, Dad recovered from his initial shock. "William—and Jessica! What a surprise!" He came over and took her arm as though to lead her into his office. She brushed his hand away.

"I didn't come to see you, Gregory. I'm here on other business."

Dad affected joviality. "Not come to see me? Why, Jessica, in all my years here, you've never visited my place of work, and now—"

Aunt Jessica put a finger up to her lips. "Gregory, I've no time for games and nonsense. Please quit trying to distract me as though I were senile or something."

Dad, abashed, let his hands fall to his sides. He looked at me questioningly. Aunt Jessica intercepted the look.

"I have asked William to accompany me on this bit of business. I shall take responsibility."

Dad was silent for a moment, his eyes reflecting struggle. "Very well. Mrs. Preston, would you see if Mr. Nisbett can see Mrs. Brassey?"

"Yes, sir." Mrs. Preston didn't like it. That was evi-

167

dent in the jerky motion of her hands as she pretended to rearrange some papers on her desk before going to knock on Mr. Nisbett's door.

The three of us looked at one another. "Jessica," Dad said rapidly under his breath, "I hope you know what you're doing—and I also hope you remember that I'm employed here."

"Don't worry, Gregory. If he fires you, you can come to work at the bookstore."

Dad opened his mouth to argue, but just then Mr. Nisbett appeared in the office doorway. His expression was inscrutable, but whatever it meant, I didn't like it. I wanted to turn and leave quietly. I needed to be in the Riverton High School cafeteria hanging crepe paper and festoons of ribbon from the rafters.

Mr. Nisbett cleared his throat, lowered his chin, and peered at us over the tops of his rimless spectacles. He looked at Dad for an explanation, but Dad remained silent.

"Good afternoon, Mr. Nisbett," said Aunt Jessica.

"Good afternoon, Mrs. Brassey."

I looked down at my feet, sideways at the dull walls, overhead at the cracking plaster ceiling, and understood how a worm in hot ashes must feel. The collar of my shirt seemed much too tight for such a warm day.

Mrs. Preston's voice was quavery. "Mrs. Brassey was wondering if you could spare her a few minutes?"

"I suppose so." It was clear he wasn't happy about it. "You will step into my office, please?"

"Thank you. Come, William."

Mr. Nisbett almost balked then. He didn't want me in his office, but how could he ask me to wait outside? I wanted to help him by excusing myself and leaving immediately, but curiosity and Aunt Jessica's determination held me. I followed her into the office, avoiding Dad's eyes.

"You may sit here." Mr. Nisbett indicated a chair. "And you, William, there."

The chair he offered her was a large comfortable leather beast with broad arms and soft cushions, but she sat poised as though it were covered with spikes. I was on a wooden stool behind her, grateful to be out of the way.

Mr. Nisbett took his seat behind the desk. "Now. What did you want to see me about?"

Aunt Jessica got straight to the point. "You must know that Kate Benson is my good friend?"

Mr. Nisbett's face closed tighter than ever. "Mrs. Brassey, I must interrupt. A trial is pending and any discussion of . . . er . . . the business to which it relates is likely to jeopardize the outcome. You, of all people, ought to realize that."

"Jeopardize the outcome for whom, Mr. Nisbett?"

"For everyone concerned, Mrs. Brassey."

"I think not. There has to be some possibility of gain or loss for jeopardy to be an issue. Kate has nothing to gain or lose at this point. Therefore I wish to speak."

Mr. Nisbett was both puzzled and piqued. He leaned forward and rested his arms on the desk. "Very well, if I can't stop you. However, I hope you are aware of your responsibility to Cousin Kate. Anything you say could be used against her cause."

"I have considered all those things."

It sounded strange to hear Mr. Nisbett call Mrs. Benson "Cousin Kate." I wondered if that was something new. He leaned back in the chair once more, prepared to listen.

"First of all," said Aunt Jessica, "you may or may not know that Kate has decided to go back to California. She intends to do nothing to contest the suit. Against the advice of her lawyers she intends to give up all claim to Edgar Benson's money and property."

Mr. Nisbett's eyes positively glazed over. "What do you mean? Why hasn't she told me of this?"

"She will, probably this very afternoon."

"I think it extremely forward of you, Mrs. Brassey, to come gossiping about a matter of such importance! I'm sure if Cousin Kate knew you had violated her confidence, she would be very angry, not to say hurt."

Aunt Jessica nodded. "That's true. I am risking the loss of her friendship, and that, sir, is no small thing."

The room seemed too small to contain the feeling within it. I thought longingly of being hidden under a table or in a cupboard.

"Now, I have some more things to tell you. When Kate married Edgar Benson she was no poverty-stricken schoolteacher. She was a woman of property. She owned a cattle ranch that had been willed to her by her father. She also owned profitable realty. She signed over all of it to Edgar when they were married. Her property became his, according to the one-sided law of this land."

Mr. Nisbett could no longer hide his amazement. I'm sure my face and his must have looked much the same. "Why wasn't I told about this?"

"I suppose she thought it was a matter between her and Edgar and was none of your business."

Mr. Nisbett accepted the chastisement because he could not do otherwise.

"In recent years Edgar became very tightfisted, as you may or may not know," said Aunt Jessica. "Most people, I believe, did *not* know it. He went about in an expensive car, the house was full of servants, he continued to hold dinner parties and entertainments. I believe if you know anything about the business affairs of St. Bartholomew's, however, you will discover that he made no contribution to his church for the past three years. Nor to charity. Worse than that, though, he came to the point where he refused to disburse funds to buy food for the table or to pay the servants' wages."

"Incredible!" Mr. Nisbett burst out. "I don't believe you!"

"I can prove everything I have said, if need be," she said calmly. "Hear me out. Kate was reduced to borrowing money from a . . . friend in order to pay the grocer and the servants. She could not borrow from a bank because to do so would have required the doctor's signature, since all their property was in his name. He refused to sign anything, saying she was after his money, and that all she wanted was for him to die so she could get it. He said the servants were her hirelings and were conspiring against him. He threatened often to alter his will. He would, he said, leave his money to someone who cared about him. But of course no one cared more for him than Kate. If it were not so, she would have left him long ago."

Mr. Nisbett made some sort of growling noise in the back of his throat, but did not interrupt. Aunt Jessica leaned forward, resting her hands upon the umbrella handle.

"Paul, your cousin Edgar was a difficult man. Kate lived in the appearance of luxury, but the truth was, she lived on less than *I* do. She had nothing. She has bought no new clothes for herself in more than three years. She has not been able to travel to visit her

171

relatives because Edgar would not give her the money. I will tell you something else: Kate knows how important Edgar was to this town. He was held in high esteem. He put this town on the map, so to speak. She will not do anything to tarnish that image of him—not even for her own well-being or in her own defense. She does not want him proved senile, demented, or incompetent.

"No doubt you can prove in court that he was all those things. He *was,* God knows! But who put up with his strange behavior? Certainly not you, nor I. If in some lucid moment Edgar Benson was able to realize that his greatest treasure was Kate Benson, and that she of all people deserved what he had denied her in his lifetime, then I'm sorry it cannot stand!"

Aunt Jessica drew a long, tremulous breath. Right then I would have put her up against William Jennings Bryan.

She stood. "That's all I have to say. I could not bear for Kate to leave this town tomorrow under a cloud, with no one knowing what she has borne these past few years."

Mr. Nisbett seemed subdued. He stood too, came around his desk, and held out his hand.

"Thank you, Mrs. Brassey." His voice had lost its hard edge.

Aunt Jessica took the proffered hand, pumped it once, brusquely. Then with a nod to me she opened the door for herself and went out. I followed behind her, mumbling good-by to Mr. Nisbett.

Dad was waiting in the outer office, but Aunt Jessica scarcely looked in his direction. She was like an old general, weighed down by the sadness of many campaigns. Dad touched my shoulder as I passed by, but what could I tell him? I turned my palms upward and shrugged as I followed in her wake.

Outside in the bare Gin yard she stopped long enough to consult the watch. "It's three o'clock, William. I expect you have things to do to get ready for the Commencement exercises tonight. You may have the rest of the afternoon off."

"Well, Bull and I do have some more decorating to do, unless he's finished by now. I should go back to help, if you're sure—"

"Yes. And I want you not to repeat any of what you heard this afternoon."

"Don't worry! Just thinking about it makes me tired."

"And well it should!" she said. "I shall see you at the auditorium tonight."

I watched for a short while as her broad figure retreated down the street. The words she had uttered in Mr. Nisbett's office had rung like fine oratory, but every sentence of it, I knew, was truth. Aunt Jessica was as honest as Jesus. It was impossible not to admire her.

I touched the box under my shirt. Something inside me shrank and hid.

18

SCHOOL HAD LET OUT for the summer and the streets were full of laughing kids all ages. No more pencils, no more books, no more teachers' dirty looks.

"Hey, Will!" someone called. "You're going the wrong way. School's out!"

"Yeah, I know! I forgot something!" I went around the side of the building to the cafeteria. Bull and the crew had finished without me. Everything appeared to be in readiness—the tables covered with white linen, the crepe paper streamers hanging from wires and light fixtures, the wooden chairs lined along the walls. The fragrance of fresh-cut flowers did not quite drown the ghost of vegetable soup, but no one would notice tonight.

I sat in one of the chairs and leaned my head back against the wall. The cafeteria was cool and quiet. I stayed until I no longer heard voices in the school yard, then got up and went out.

The auditorium was across a courtyard from the cafeteria. I went up the outside fire escape to the backstage door. It was still and dark in the auditorium, and at first I thought no one was there, but when I reached the second set of steps leading to the

174

stage, I heard voices and someone walking around. I slipped off my shoes before going up. Since the only thing separating me from the voices was the thick beige curtain that hung at the rear of the stage, I ducked behind some wooden crates to listen.

"That looks wonderful!" Lilly's voice said. "Where did you ever find such a beautiful banner?"

"My father knew someone." Although the curtains muffled the voice, I recognized it as Paul's.

"Well," said Lilly, "I believe we've taken care of everything. I'm going to leave this box of awards under the speaker's lectern for the time being. I'll come early tonight and arrange them on the table in the right order."

"You think it's O.K. to leave them here?"

"Of course! They're of no use to anyone except the people who win them."

"That's true. I suppose people would get suspicious if the class dummy went around with the Latin medal pinned to his shirt."

They laughed at that. I listened as they went down from the stage and out into the auditorium. Shortly the doors opened and shut, then all was silent. I found a break in the beige curtain and peeped through. The large maroon velvet curtain at the front of the stage was open. The speakers' chairs had been arranged in two rows. There was the table for the awards and diplomas, and tall arrangements of flowers at each end of the stage. In the very center stood the speaker's lectern, and in the gloom I could see the large cardboard box on the little shelf underneath. I touched the bulge under my shirt.

Thinking it would be smart to close the velvet curtains before switching the boxes, I made my way around to the ropes and pulled until I found the right one. Unfortunately, I discovered a second too late that the tall baskets of flowers were in line with the curtain. They crashed in unison as the heavy material dragged by them.

Frantically, I ran to set the baskets upright. The jars that fitted inside them had spilled their contents upon the stage—two slow, creeping puddles of water. Luckily, the flowers had been stuck into those gadgets with holes that Mother calls frogs. The stems stayed in the holes, so I didn't have to rearrange the flowers.

By the time I had found a rag to wipe the spill and had replaced the water in the jars, I was shaking like a bum with the d.t.'s. I should have taken that incident as a sign that my luck was turning sour, but by then I was obsessed with the notion of switching the two boxes. I had gone through so much to bring it off, I couldn't give it up.

So I pulled the cardboard box from the lectern and set it on the floor. Taking care to keep the little boxes in the proper order, I lifted them out one by one until I came at last to The One. Quickly I unbuttoned my shirt and took out its twin, made the switch, tucked the "real" box into my shirt, replaced the others, and put the large box back in its place under the lectern. No one would suspect a thing. What a perfect joke!

Suddenly I heard the door open at the back of the auditorium. For a brief instant I was frozen, then I broke and ran for all I was worth across the stage, behind the beige curtain, down the steps, and out the fire escape exit. Squinting against the sun's glare, I clattered down the metal steps to the ground and cut across the back side of the school yard. I did not stop until I had reached a shady spot on a back street two and a half blocks away. Perspiration streamed from

176

my forehead and neck, and my heart was pounding so I thought my chest was going to explode. I leaned against a wooden fence to catch my breath, aware that my legs were trembling.

I kept waiting for the feeling of elation I had expected when the deed was accomplished. It didn't come. Instead, all I could think of was how I would feel if I had been expecting the history medal and opened the box to find a 1918 Sunday school pin. But Paul was always getting medals and awards. He was used to it. It wouldn't be such a big deal to him, would it?

I came to our house quietly, having walked as slowly as I could without actually loitering. Dinner smells floated out into the hallway. I felt nauseated. I tiptoed upstairs and lay down across the bed. Every nerve throbbed with the tension of the afternoon. The box under my shirt dug into my belly, a sharp reminder of what I had done.

I rolled over and sat up, pulling the box out of my shirt. Its paper was slightly damp. What to do with it? I considered opening it then and there. I wanted to see what the new medal looked like. No doubt it was engraved with Paul's name and Lilly had already seen it. In the end, though, I left it wrapped and hid it in the rear corner of the highest wardrobe drawer in G.C.'s room. Mother would have to stand on a chair to see the inside of that drawer, so the box was safe until tomorrow, when I would mail it to Paul.

"William, is that you?" Mother called from downstairs.

"Yes, ma'am."

"Aren't you home early?"

"Aunt Jessica gave me the afternoon off. I've been over at the school, finishing up."

"Bull Clammett came by about an hour ago and said he had already finished. He wanted to know where you were."

"Yeah—that's right. I missed him. But I still had a couple of things to do. I'm going to take a bath now. I have to be back at the school by seven."

"All right. We'll have dinner as soon as your father gets home."

I think I had hoped that a bath and fresh clothes would restore my enthusiasm for what was to come, but they only cooled me off. I put on my gray Sunday suit, hot and scratchy as it was, and went down to dinner. I caught a glimpse of myself in the hall mirror, somber-faced and a trifle pale.

"You look nice!" Mother said, beaming with approval. "So mature. It's hard to believe that my baby boy is already grown up."

I made a face. I hate to hear her talk like that.

"Well!" exclaimed Dad when he came in a few minutes later. "How nice you look!"

"Thank you, sir." I stood there uncomfortably while he looked me over and straightened my tie to suit him. For years I had wanted to see on his face the expression of pleasure I saw there now. For once he was satisfied with me—and of all the times in my life, I knew I least deserved his approval now. I wished it was tomorrow—or yesterday.

"You look pale, William," Mother said. "Are you sure you feel all right?"

I nodded. "I think I got too hot this afternoon coming home."

"Or," said Dad, "could it have something to do with the excitement in Mr. Nisbett's office?"

Curiously, it seemed to me that the person who had gone with Aunt Jessica was not me at all, but

178

some other guy who looked like me and was a lot nicer. Seeing the puzzled look on Mother's face, Dad told her what had happened. I remembered Aunt Jessica's injunction and kept my mouth shut.

When we went in to dinner, the odor of food nearly overwhelmed me. I did not think I could manage a single bite, but conscious of Mother's worried looks I made myself eat.

"Mr. Nisbett called me in just before closing time," Dad announced with the air of a person who has great news to tell. "He asked whether I had had anything to do with Jessica's sudden appearance this afternoon. I assured him that I did not—that I had, in fact, tried to dissuade her. He said he did not doubt that. 'Your sister,' he said—and I think with some awe, though I'll never tell *her* so—'is not the ordinary sort of woman.' "

He and Mother laughed together at that. I managed a grin, just to be in the mood of things.

"He said, 'I want you to tell her, for me, that I have decided not to contest Cousin Edgar's will—and that I hope she's satisfied.' "

Mother gave a little shriek of undisguised joy and clasped her hands under her chin.

"Isn't that splendid?" Dad looked from Mother to me with such a self-satisfied expression you would have thought that he and not Aunt Jessica was responsible. I laid my fork on my plate, about 95 percent sure that I was lying upstairs on my bed dreaming crazy things. Nothing seemed real.

"Are you sure?" Even my voice belonged to someone else.

"Absolutely. He told me that he had telephoned his lawyers and advised them to contact Mrs. Benson immediately. Then he said he was going to call on

179

her this very evening, to see if he could persuade her not to leave Riverton."

I contemplated all this with a strange detachment. Maybe people felt like this when they knew they were going to die—vaguely curious but too tired to be involved.

"You know," said Dad, "Mr. Nisbett has climbed several notches in my estimation. I admire a man who, when he's made a mistake, can turn and correct it before serious damage is done."

I pushed my food around with my fork. "Did you tell Aunt Jessica?"

"I came by her house on my way home. When I told her, she said, 'Praise the Lord!' and burst into tears."

Mother gaped. "Jessica burst into tears?"

"Yes," said Dad. "It's certainly a day of miracles, isn't it?"

Not the least of which is the one you're going to see tonight, I thought miserably. I wished that Riverton High School's Commencement exercises were not such a big community affair. No one missed a graduation unless sick or infirm. Parents, grandparents, uncles, aunts, cousins, friends, brothers, sisters—Riverton was One Great Family. G.C., Aunt Jessica, Mother, and Dad would be there. We would sit together, and when Paul Nisbett opened his "history medal" they would know immediately by what Miracle it came to be transformed into a 1918 Sunday school perfect attendance pin. The approving person my dad had become would turn distant and cold again. Mother would be hurt, Aunt Jessica disappointed, G.C. scornful. The saddest part was that I knew none of them would be surprised. Hoping a person has changed doesn't make it so.

"I have to be going. I'm supposed to be there at seven." I pushed back my chair and stood up.

"But you hardly ate a thing," Mother protested.

"I—think it's because I'm nervous about whether everything will go the way we planned. This is the first time the junior class has helped, you know."

"Of course." Dad smiled. "Shall we save you a seat?"

"Yes, sir. I'll see you there."

I left the house pursued by the image of their innocence smiling under the light of the dining room chandelier.

19

THE RIVERTON HIGH SCHOOL auditorium was ablaze with lights. The still, hot air held the odor of gardenias and chewing tobacco, peppermint and onions, cloves and sweat. The banner that Paul had brought hung the full width of the stage lauding "RIVERTON HIGH SCHOOL CLASS OF 1923" in vivid red on white. The place was packed, except for the fifty empty seats reserved at the front by wide red and white satin ribbon. Upon the stage the table covered in white cloth held diplomas for seniors and awards for members of all the high school classes. It was an impressive sight, I thought dolefully, sweating in my gray suit between Aunt Jessica and Mother. Dad sat on the other side of Mother, and G.C. and Dolores beside him. We took up nearly half the row.

Everything looked complete and orderly. Thanks to Lilly, the class of '23 would be graduated in grand style. I took little pleasure in remembering that it had been my idea. A single box up there on the table virtually glowed with its mischievous contents. I sighed and squirmed.

"Sit still, William," Aunt Jessica commanded. "Wiggling will only make you hot."

She had been saying that to me since I was three.

182

I wondered whether she realized I was almost sixteen.

She turned her head and caught me studying her. A wisp of a smile touched her mouth and disappeared. "Thank you for going with me this afternoon. It seems the visit bore fruit. I don't know whether I could have done it without you."

"Aw, Aunt Jessica—that's blarney!"

"That shows how little you know. You realize, of course, why I took you?"

"Frankly, no. I thought maybe you wanted to teach me a lesson or something. *I* don't know."

Aunt Jessica chuckled, and her plump body shook all over. "A lesson? My stars, William. I can't believe you of all people would be so naive!"

"Why did you take me, then?"

"I needed a witness, of course!"

"But why didn't you get Dad to go with you—or a lawyer?"

"It wouldn't have done at all. I needed someone who could remember the exchange and the significance of it, but who would in no way present a threat to Mr. Nisbett's view of himself. He didn't have to show off for you. You were the perfect one." She looked at me in a worried way. "You don't mind terribly, do you?"

"Mind? Of course not! I'm flattered."

She smiled, and I thought ruefully that perhaps I had come by my scheming genes honestly. All I had to learn now was what to scheme *for*.

The piano at the front of the auditorium began a rather stormy rendition of Handel's "Largo" and the audience rose to its feet. The fifty graduating seniors and the speakers made their way with dignity down the two aisles. The girls were dressed in white and

183

carried red roses. The boys wore dark suits. Watching them, I had a strange, lost feeling. Next year this time I would be in that line. I gazed around me to keep from looking at the slow-moving column and saw the Nisbetts standing across the aisle from us. Mrs. Benson was with them, tears glistening on her cheeks. I suppose she was remembering the boys and girls she once taught. I wished I was outside somewhere in the cooler air.

At last the seniors had filed into the rows of reserved seats and the speakers were in front of their chairs on the stage. Then everyone sat in a great, rumbling sigh. There were a lot of speakers—the valedictorian of the class and the salutatorian; the class president; Miss Lauderbach; the Reverend Duncan; Mr. Bailey, the principal; the chairman of the school board; and the main speaker, who was a renowned professor of history at a nearby university. As the evening wore on I had more than ample time to reflect on what I had done and what was about to happen. In this setting, among eager relatives and parents, the anticipation of my joke had perished like a man under a mustard gas attack. I kept thinking about Dad's words at dinner: *I admire a man who, when he's made a mistake, can turn and correct it before serious damage is done.*

Turn and correct it. How the heck could I turn and correct it? The fake box lay on the table in front of eight hundred people. The real box lay in the rear of a wardrobe drawer two blocks away. There was no way, now, to prevent the damage.

Unless, when Paul was called up to receive the award, I stood and confessed what I had done to this crowd of people.

The thought made me literally sick. I swallowed

184

hard several times and sank lower in my seat. The speaker uttered words I did not hear.

"William, you look ill," said Aunt Jessica without lowering her voice. "Do you want to go outside?"

I shook my head. The people in the row in front of us turned their heads to look at me. I stared straight ahead and pretended to be absorbed in the speaker's words.

At long last the speaker sat down and there was an enthusiastic burst of applause, probably from the audience's joy that he was through. Now we were at the part everyone had come to see—the giving out of awards and diplomas. Miss Lauderbach came forward to the lectern. In a strong, firm voice that carried all the way to the rear of the auditorium she began to explain the value of excellence. Excellence, she said with conviction, is its own reward.

"The young men and women who will receive these awards tonight have gone beyond what was required of them. They have demonstrated excellence in many fields. Some will receive several awards. Some will receive one. The quantity does not matter. It is quality that counts."

The crowd applauded her words. "I shall begin with the eighth-grade freshman class, then the sophomores, then juniors, and finally the seniors. At this time I should like to call Miss Lilly Fentrice of the junior class to the stage to assist me with the awards."

Lilly came out on the stage. She was wearing a soft pale-yellow dress, and her brown hair glistened under the lights. I opened and shut my eyes a time or two, to be sure that wonderful-looking creature was really Lilly.

"Before we begin," said Miss Lauderbach, "I should like to say to you all that this young lady has

185

been of inestimable help to me in the past two weeks." She went on to tell all that Lilly had done, and ended by saying, "As a result of the tremendous help I received from the junior class through Lilly's fine organizing, we shall have a committee from the juniors each year to take this responsibility. I want us all to give Lilly and the juniors a big hand, to show our appreciation."

I yelled and clapped louder than anyone. At least one good thing had come out of my scheme.

The awards began. Each name called brought rounds of applause and cheers. The recipient had to go up from the audience to the stage and shake Miss Lauderbach's hand. I kept glancing over at Paul, imagining, as his name was called for the history medal, his starting forward, and my jumping up and shrieking a confession, and my father and mother and aunt and brother shrinking in embarrassment. I couldn't do it.

"The following awards are presented to members of the junior class," Miss Lauderbach intoned. "As I call your name, please come forward."

There was the Brent Athletic Award to the best all-around athlete in the junior class. Paul Nisbett was the recipient.

And the Music Medal, presented to the glee club member who had made the most outstanding contribution to the club and school. Paul Nisbett.

And the French Medal, to the outstanding French II student. Paul Nisbett.

There were other awards of course that Paul did not receive, but only because he wasn't eligible, such as the Home Economics prize and the Orchestra Medal and some others like that. As the list went on I began to hope that perhaps, by some wonderful and remote stroke of Fate, the history medal had been misplaced.

"And now," said Miss Lauderbach, "it is with great pride that I announce the winner of a new award. This prize is the Douglas History Award, presented by *The Riverton Courier* to the individual in our school who submits the best paper on some topic of history, recent or ancient. The papers were judged by the members of the History Department of Riverton High School, by the editors of *The Riverton Courier,* and by tonight's speaker, Dr. Harry D. Winton of Bacon University. The winner of this award will receive an engraved medal and have his name inscribed on a plaque that will remain on display in the school's halls at all times. Each year the name of another deserving recipient will be added. We are grateful to *The Riverton Courier* for making this award possible."

Miss Lauderbach paused and shuffled through some papers on the lectern before her. I thought I would leap out of my skin. My eyes were riveted upon Paul Nisbett.

"The winner of this year's Douglas History Award is—*William Thomas!*"

I was lifted up on waves of noisy cheers, and I heard myself shouting "No!" Friendly hands pushed me as I stumbled over feet and out into the aisle. I caught a glimpse of Dad's broad smile, of Mother's happy tears. I couldn't stop shaking my head. Something was wrong. I looked dumbly at Paul as I passed. He was grinning from ear to ear.

The aisle was interminable. My legs threatened to fold. My mind raced my feet to the stage, to the moment when the offending box would be safe in my hands. In my extreme relief I offered up a promise that as soon as I paid Bull back the two dollars I owed him, I was going to put an extra fifty cents in the church collection plate.

On stage at last, I shook Miss Lauderbach's hand, endured her look of pride, and reached for the oh-so-familiar box. She held it deftly just out of my reach.

"William, we are very proud of you. Professor Winton has remarked to me that your paper showed remarkable maturity of thought and execution. He predicts that if this is typical of the work you do, you will go far."

I heard a few snickers in the audience. I am well known in Riverton.

"Since this is the first time this medal has been awarded, I'd like you to open it right here and read to the audience the inscription engraved upon it."

If I had thought I felt sick before, it was as nothing to the nausea that overwhelmed me in that moment. I stared at Miss Lauderbach, and then past her at Lilly, who was smiling confidently at me. I was trapped. Five minutes before I had thought the Almighty had rescued me. Now I realized He had only been saving me for the Big Guns.

I swallowed, licked my dry lips, and began with trembling fingers to undo the red ribbon I had tied and to tear away the paper I had glued. Finally the bare box lay in my hand. I lifted the lid.

There, nestled in velvet, gleamed a silver medal upon a red satin ribbon. It read: "Douglas History Award. For outstanding achievement in historical scholarship. William Bennington Thomas. 1923."

How?

A day of miracles, Dad had said. Perhaps one did not question a miracle. I took this one with more gratitude, humility, and shame than I ever dreamed

188

was in me. I read the inscription aloud in a thin, reedy voice to a quiet audience. And then I closed the box and shook Miss Lauderbach's hand again— and she kissed my cheek! And then all pandemonium broke loose. Miss Lauderbach probably hadn't kissed a male in public in her whole life. Yells, catcalls, belly laughs, cheers, stamping. I don't know how I found my way back to the seat between Mother and Aunt Jessica. G.C. pounded me on the back. Dad was ecstatic. Throughout the rest of the exercises he kept reaching over to pat me on the knee. Aunt Jessica was the only person who seemed pleased but not surprised.

When it was over the audience rose while the senior class sang the alma mater with subdued voices, and then as they marched out, the piano played the melody over and over. My face felt held together by safety pins and glue.

At the end, as everyone crowded into the aisles, Bull and Paul converged on either side of me, each one putting an arm across my shoulders. The three of us blocked the aisle.

"I really thought you were going to pull one," Bull said in one ear. "I'm sorry I've been such a jackass these last couple of weeks."

"Forget it," I said fervently. "Pals?"

"Pals!" We shook on it.

"Thank God you got that damned history medal!" Paul said in the other ear. "If I'd gotten another, I think I would've donated it to the Salvation Army!"

The three of us laughed and horsed around all the way to the cafeteria. I knew I was laughing too loud and acting insane, but what else does a guy do who has been saved just when he was going down for the third time?

Lilly was the person I looked for, but it was several minutes before I found her standing on the edge of the crowd, looking tired but satisfied. She had reason to be satisfied. She certainly did look fine in that yellow dress.

When she saw me her face lighted up, which served to raise the soles of my shoes about three inches off the floor.

"Congratulations, Will! I'm so proud."

"Lilly, . . . I have something to tell you—"

She toyed with the catch on her purse and, looking around to be sure no one was noticing, she took from it a familiar box and slipped it into my hand. "Put it in your pocket," she ordered.

"How'd you know?" I asked, ashamed and abashed before her, but oh, so grateful.

"You're transparent," she told me. "You were so interested in knowing about that particular one, remember? And your competition with Paul wasn't too well hidden, you know. I knew you were up to something from the beginning. That's why I volunteered to chair the committee, so I could head you off. I kept that medal in my purse until this very night. Then I took the box that was there and left the right one."

I shook my head in admiration. "Did Paul know?"

"Of course not! Do you think I'd spoil the chance for you and him to be friends someday?"

"No, I guess not. But why didn't you let me go ahead and fall flat on my face? If anyone ever deserved it, I do."

"Will Thomas, you're such a dummy!" Lilly stamped her foot, exasperated. "Can't you tell when someone loves you?"

Red cheeks. Flashing eyes.

Then she realized what she had said, and her old

shyness came back in a rush. Her hand covered her mouth. It was my turn to take charge, and I did. I leaned over, removed the hand, and gave her a resounding smack on the lips. She did not faint.

It was, indeed, a day of Miracles.

ABOUT THE AUTHOR

SUZANNE NEWTON was born in Bunnlevel, Harnett County, North Carolina, and lived in several villages and towns before settling in Raleigh, in 1960.

Mrs. Newton graduated from Duke University in 1957 and taught English and French in Clarkton, North Carolina, for two years. She is married to Carl Newton and they have three daughters—Michele, Erin, and Heather—and a son, Craig. "All are avid readers," she says. "Music and books are staples of our family life."

Writing, for Mrs. Newton, is an adventure in self-discovery. For her, writing is not plotting and manipulating, but digging, discovery, and involvement.